THE FARMHOUSE COUNTRY COOKBOOK

THE FARMHOUSE COUNTRY COOKBOOK

170 traditional recipes shown in
680 evocative step-by-step photographs

SARAH BANBERY

greene&golden

This edition is published by greene&golden,
an imprint of Anness Publishing Ltd, Blaby Road, Wigston,
Leicestershire LE18 4SE; info@anness.com

www.annesspublishing.com

If you like the images in this book and would like to
investigate using them for publishing, promotions or
advertising, please visit our website
www.practicalpictures.com for more information.

Publisher: Joanna Lorenz
Project Editors: Amy Christian and Felicity Forster
Copy Editor: Catherine Best
Designer: Design Principals
Recipes: Pepita Aris, Catherine Atkinson, Alex Barker,
   Ghillie Basan, Georgina Campbell, Carla Capalbo,
   Miguel de Castro e Silva, Lesley Chamberlain,
   Carole Clements, Matthew Drennan, Jenni Fleetwood,
   Brian Glover, Christine Ingram, Bridget Jones, Lucy Knox,
   Janet Laurence, Sally Mansfield, Maggie Mayhew,
   Anna Mosesson, Keith Richmond, Rena Salaman,
   Jennie Shapter, Christopher Trotter, Suzanne Vandyck,
   Laura Washburn, Biddy White Lennon, Carol Wilson,
   Annette Yates
Photographers: Nicki Dowey, Ian Garlick,
   Amanda Heywood, Janine Hosegood, Dave Jordan,
   William Lingwood, Steve Moss, Craig Robertson
Production Controller: Wendy Lawson

© Anness Publishing Ltd 2012

A CIP catalogue record for this book is available from
the British Library.

NOTES

Bracketed terms are intended for American readers.
For all recipes, quantities are given in both metric and
imperial measures and, where appropriate, in standard
cups and spoons. Follow one set of measures, but not
a mixture, because they are not interchangeable.
Standard spoon and cup measures are level.
1 tsp = 5ml, 1 tbsp = 15ml, 1 cup = 250ml/8fl oz.
Australian standard tablespoons are 20ml. Australian
readers should use 3 tsp in place of 1 tbsp for measuring
small quantities.
American pints are 16fl oz/2 cups. American readers
should use 20fl oz/2.5 cups in place of 1 pint when
measuring liquids.
Electric oven temperatures in this book are for conventional
ovens. When using a fan oven, the temperature will
probably need to be reduced by about 10–20°C/20–40°F.
Since ovens vary, you should check with your
manufacturer's instruction book for guidance.
The nutritional analysis given for each recipe is calculated
per portion (i.e. serving or item), unless otherwise stated.
If the recipe gives a range, such as Serves 4–6, then the
nutritional analysis will be for the smaller portion size,
i.e. 6 servings. The analysis does not include optional
ingredients, such as salt added to taste.
Medium (US large) eggs are used unless otherwise stated.

Front cover image shows Old-fashioned Deep-dish
Apple Pie – for recipe, see pages 197.

PUBLISHER'S NOTE

CONTENTS

Introduction

Country cooking is essentially based on traditional peasant food that has evolved over the centuries. The authentic recipes of the countryside naturally rely on good ingredients and fresh seasonal produce, making use of all the fantastic richness of locally produced food throughout the year. Peasant and country dishes also include many more esoteric foods such as oysters and game which are today regarded as luxury items, but in the past would actually have been classified as poor man's food.

The hard-won knowledge and frugal habits of the country cook, developed with patience and skill over time, are reflected in our 21st-century concerns with the origin and provenance of ingredients. We are beginning to understand that local, fresh, seasonal produce has a better flavour and is far more nutritionally rich than food that is imported from far-flung countries out of season, and this is an area where country recipes shine.

The age-old custom of passing down tried-and-tested traditional family recipes from generation to generation, along with cherished cooking skills, equipment and utensils, means that country food has survived to be appreciated and enjoyed by each new generation of cooks.

The contemporary country kitchen

With a growing interest in cooking seasonally, in using organic produce and the simplest, freshest ingredients, the contemporary country kitchen retains much of what is best about traditional cooking, but with the added blessing of modern equipment, time-saving gadgets and appliances. Innovations such as pressure cookers and bread machines mean that the busy home cook can now recreate many of the more time-consuming recipes of the past in a fraction of the time, without losing any authentic taste. In modern kitchens, it is easier than ever to make the most of all the fresh, high-quality ingredients on which country cooking is based.

Home-made food

Country cooking is simply delicious home-made food using traditional raw materials, without any unnecessary waste. For example, many meat dishes involve long, slow cooking, making use of every possible part of an animal such as the trotters, the head and the offal. This thrifty custom has played a key role in developing some of the best-loved country meat recipes.

An integral part of this style of cooking was preserving food, which was an absolute necessity rather than an indulgence. Home baking and home smoking, along with pickling and salting, and making cheese and butter, were a natural part of living in the country and a matter of pride. Many a country larder contained neat rows of preserved fruit and vegetables in jars, with maybe a ham or some game hanging on a hook and a crock of salted fish ready to be eaten in the cold

Left Summer in the country means rich grazing for farm animals and an abundance of produce from the woods, fields and vegetable plot.

months of winter. Techniques such as making a rich stock from meat bones or vibrant crab apple jelly from windfall fruits illustrate the inventiveness that characterizes much country cooking.

The seasons

Culinary creativity was very important to the country cook, whose life revolved around the seasons. Traditional recipes tended to be structured around one central ingredient which was in season – spring vegetables tasting wonderful in a delicious soup, or pork as the main ingredient of a raised pie, for example. If there was an abundance of one crop, it was either used fresh in different ways or stored for the cold weather.

Spring could still be a time of year when the cook was largely reliant on preserved foods to support the few early vegetables, while the summer months provided plenty of fresh fruits, vegetables and salads from an overflowing kitchen garden. In the autumn, the country cook has traditionally relied heavily on wild foods to support the larder and pantry. Game from the fields and woods, as well as hedgerow fruits and nuts, complemented the last of the

summer crops. Winter recipes reflect the thriftiness of country cooking, with hearty stews making the most of the root vegetables, brassicas and dried beans and peas, and using bottled and pickled vegetables from the store cupboard to bulk up meagre winter crops.

Country traditions

The simple act of baking a certain loaf of bread or a special cake for a specific celebration or festival evolved over time to become an indelible part of country tradition. These rituals, treasured and passed down within families, connected people both to the rhythms of the countryside and to the traditions of their local community, marking the passing of the year. Harvest suppers, spiced Christmas drinks, festival sweetmeats and Easter cakes are all concocted from ancient recipes in the country kitchen.

Today, spending time in the kitchen baking a fruit cake, chopping home-grown vegetables to make soup or cooking wonderfully nutritious food

Left Country cooking techniques often rely on a few well-loved utensils, such as this traditional rolling pin, pastry cutters, mixing bowl and jug.

Above *Home-grown local fruits such as these beautiful apples are used in many country recipes, such as a sweet pie or a savoury roast joint of meat.*

from a few simple ingredients reconnects us to the countryside. Even growing a few herbs in pots on the window sill or making your own preserves can give a satisfying feeling of keeping up time-honoured culinary customs.

About the book

This book begins with a description of country cooking, its history, methods and ingredients, including some fascinating facts about the practical cooking techniques of our rural ancestors. There is also plenty of inspiration for growing your own produce, using it wisely when fresh, and preserving the inevitable glut to enjoy in the colder months.

There are eight chapters of recipes, ranging from simple, rustic soups and pot roasts to some best-loved regional specialities, puddings, breads and preserves. Many dishes can be prepared ahead of time or slow-cooked all day in traditional fashion, bringing the real taste of the country to your table.

Country traditions

Throughout the centuries, cooks have prepared food for the family using whatever ingredients were available. Peasant cooking relied entirely on goods from the local area, fresh and in season, plus whatever could be preserved by bottling, pickling, salting or drying to eat when the kitchen garden was covered with snow and the wheat fields were bare. Today we can be inspired by the thrifty methods of the past to make delicious meals that everyone will enjoy.

The history of country cooking

The development of our traditional cooking has its roots in pre-history. The earliest cooking would probably have been limited to roasting meat and game on a spit, toasting and grinding grain and using simple hollowed-out stones and bones to heat liquids over an open fire.

Early cooking techniques

Not until the development of settled agriculture and the introduction of pottery would cooking develop beyond the most basic methods. By the Middle Ages the resourceful country cook, restricted by the limitations of one-pot cooking on an open fire, relied on tasty dishes such as soups, stews and casseroles, spit-roasted meat and preserved fruit and vegetables for many months of the year. Bread dough was baked in a central public oven, since most of the rural populace would not have access to an oven at home.

Tools, equipment and utensils

From mankind's earliest days, much effort was put into developing tools for gathering, killing and cooking food. Clay, iron and bronze materials were

fashioned into pots used for cooking over the fire and also for preserving food. Utensils made of wood and metal, such as ladles and knives, became stronger and more reliable.

Well-tested techniques for preserving food were vital. As well as preserving fruit and vegetables in glass jars or earthenware crocks, many rural homes would smoke fish and meat in the chimney or in a home-built smokery.

The cook now had access to a broader range of cooking equipment, as well as specialist dairy tools for making butter and cheese. The Victorian era saw the introduction of a huge number of new cooking utensils and mass-produced kitchen gadgets such as fancy pastry cutters, cheese graters and potato peelers.

Fires and ovens

Cooking food over an open fire is the basis upon which all subsequent cooking has developed. The earliest pot ovens, domed iron pots placed over hot hearth stones, gave way to clay or brick-lined ovens similar to today's

Left Fruits such as cranberries, together with spices and herbs, were important ingredients for preserves.

Above Cherished kitchen utensils and equipment were often passed from one generation of cooks down to the next.

pizza ovens, but until the end of the 18th century, much cooking was still done over an open fire. Iron stoves began to appear in the late 18th century, but it was not until the 'cooking machines' or closed stoves appeared in Victorian kitchens that home cooking was really revolutionized.

By the 19th century the typical farmhouse kitchen had a fireplace with a chimney and a rudimentary range with its own ovens. The Aga stove or range cooker and other coal- or wood-fired ovens used today are still associated with a more traditional cooking style; they have certain limitations, but these stoves are often much loved by their owners, who have become experts in slow-cooking skills.

Larders and pantries

Keeping food fresh was a constant concern for the country cook. Storing vegetables and fruits in a cool place on stone floors with a good circulation of air meant they lasted longer. Eventually a larder cupboard or walk-in pantry was

Left The American plantation kitchen had an open hearth for cooking, a hand-cranked meat mincer and copper pots.

constructed in every rural kitchen, as well as in many town basement kitchens. This was the ideal place to keep dairy products and meat in the best condition before the advent of refrigeration. It was also a good place for keeping dry stores of beans, peas and grains, and preserved foods and vegetables in glass or earthenware jars. Many farmhouses in dairy farming areas developed their own clean, cool dairies where the scrubbed stone floors and shelves gave the best conditions for making and storing butter and cheese.

Local markets

Markets were integral to country life and the rural economy. They developed from the basic need to barter or exchange an excess of produce. These markets became the focus of many rural communities, with people travelling long distances, often on foot, to buy and sell the essentials of life. Many towns and settlements grew up around the site of a regular market, and in some countries the right to hold a market was a highly valued privilege enshrined in writing. Although both regular markets and seasonal fairs were essentially trading institutions, they became a treasured part of the life of the country. In recent eras, when many countries have seen an increase in trade and movements of population, markets played an integral role both in the dissemination of new foods and cooking styles and in the preservation of ancient local customs.

Below Fruit, vegetables and preserves are kept cool and dry in a pantry, along with dried herbs and garlic.

Frugal food

For the earliest farmers, the earth needed to be coaxed into fertility, and their hard-won skills gradually developed over many years as a response to the challenges of living off the land. The popular image of the countryside as a bucolic and tranquil place belies the reality for rural communities all over the world; the poverty and hardship of country living has always demanded an inventive and frugal way of life. Almost all country cooking relies on good sense, forward planning, a talent for improvisation when times are hard and shared skills rooted in long experience.

Making the most of the countryside

Country economy is symbolized in the use of absolutely all parts of an animal. One or two pigs were often kept in country yards to be killed and eaten in the winter – an essential source of protein for the peasant farmer and his family. Virtually no part of the pig was thrown away: once the major cuts had been eaten as roasted joints and the lesser ones as stews, fat was rendered for lard, intestines were used for sausage cases, and hearts were stuffed and braised. In many countries of the world, pig's feet and ears are a delicacy.

Recipes using ingredients collected from the wild also bear witness to the country cook's frugal outlook. These delicious dishes include soups made from wild greens, herbs and even nettles. Game, fish, nuts and seeds were all hunted or collected to enrich and diversify the country diet. Foraging for food was considered not just a source of free ingredients, but also a positive pleasure when the day could be spent hunting or fishing, picking blackberries along a field edge or searching for mushrooms in the woods.

Economical food around the world

Around the world, peasant cuisines show a great regard for frugal economy. Since peasant food traditionally uses whatever ingredients the local land has to offer, it is always both accessible and inexpensive, and often based around a limited number of staple, hearty ingredients cooked in a single pot.

Above Good economy means taking advantage of what the fields, woods and hedgerows have to offer.

Scarcity of ingredients has led to great culinary invention in many countries, with the creation of new dishes and exciting ways to present familiar ingredients. In Turkey, for example, there are countless recipes based on the simple aubergine (eggplant), examples of which can be found in glistening deep purple piles in every market. These include the famous aubergine and tomato dish, Imam Bayildi.

Left To make the most of a pig, the meat was salted, smoked or preserved, and also made into sausages.
Right Home-grown tomatoes are perfect for cooking if you can resist eating them as soon as they are picked.

In many countries, traditional meals vary only slightly across the borders, where the climate and ingredients are similar. The peasant dishes of Germany, such as Himmel und Erde, puréed potato and apple with blood sausage, and Sauerbrauten, a sweet and sour pot roast served with dumplings and cabbage, both remain distinctively German but share a common culinary heritage with other 'peasant' foods such as Irish Stew or French Cassoulet. The technique of marinating and slow cooking the less tender cuts of meat such as the shoulder, shanks and ribs resulted in mouth-watering casseroles, pot roasts and stews.

Waste not, want not

Leftovers feature prominently in country cooking. In Italy, rice left over from a risotto would be added to soups or made into Arancini – balls of cooked rice stuffed with cheese and deep-fried. Spanish Gazpacho, Italian Pappa al Pomodoro and English Queen of Puddings were all made to use up stale bread. Pizza is the ultimate peasant dish, a flour and olive oil dough base topped with tomato sauce and whichever vegetables and cheese are available.

Sourcing ingredients today

With the rise of the grass-roots movement that promotes traditionally raised food, today's resourceful cook can take advantage of the best their country has to offer. Financial imperatives paired with an increased desire to buy good, natural food means that many people are more educated about where their food comes from and what they should pay for it. Awareness of the amount of pesticides used in commercially grown crops and the less welcome effects of agro-chemicals and antibiotics used to rear livestock intensively means that many people are beginning to buy

organic and bio-dynamic foods instead. In particular, the furore over the advent of genetically modified crops has starkly illustrated the number of artificial processes associated with modern food production. In contrast, vegetable and fruit varieties grown organically may take longer to grow and have lower yields of uneven-sized crops, but they have time to develop more flavour and are nutritionally richer.

The reintroduction of traditional and rare-breed animals and an increased concern for animal welfare means that

Left A thick slice of home-baked bread, such as this cheese and onion loaf, is a delicious and filling country snack.

many more livestock and poultry are raised free-range and slaughtered in more humane conditions. Meat can often be sourced from farmers as many rural producers now sell direct to the consumer. Buying a whole or half animal from a farmer, butchered into convenient portions and ready for the freezer, means fantastic meat at a reasonable price.

Growing your own is the best way of ensuring freshness, but there are also increased opportunities for sourcing frugal ingredients. Farmers' markets, farm shops, co-operatives and box schemes offer locally grown and organic supplies which are, by definition, in season and fresh. Buying food from the person who grew or raised it has the added benefit of the exchange of knowledge, ideas and perhaps even recipes. In this way, the city-dwelling cook with an interest in traditional food can bridge the gap between urban and rural life.

Below Free-range meat from animals such as these sheep can be sourced direct from farmers and markets.

The country kitchen

Country recipes rely on traditional cooking techniques
combined with the quality and freshness of good produce.
Focusing on natural, seasonal ingredients will enable any
cook to produce wholesome food which is both healthy and
delicious. This chapter gives an overview of all the basic
ingredients used in country cooking, from the familiar fruits
and vegetables of the kitchen garden to autumn berries and
nuts, and from meat and dairy products to fish and shellfish.

Soups and appetizers

A warming bowl of home-made soup with some crusty bread and a chunk of cheese is a staple lunch or supper, relying, like most country cooking, on good seasonal ingredients. Using a home-made stock makes all the difference. Country pâtés and terrines make the most of off-cuts and can be made with a wide variety of meat and game. They are irresistible when served with home-made pickles.

Country minestrone

The famous Italian country soup from Lombardy is made with small pasta, beans and vegetables, which can include whatever ingredients are at hand from the store cupboard.

Serves 4

45ml/3 tbsp olive oil

115g/4oz pancetta, any rinds removed, roughly chopped

2–3 celery sticks, finely chopped

3 medium carrots, finely chopped

1 medium onion, finely chopped

1–2 garlic cloves, crushed

2 x 400g/14oz cans chopped tomatoes

about 1 litre/1¾ pints/4 cups chicken stock

400g/14oz can cannellini beans, drained and rinsed

50g/2oz/½ cup short–cut macaroni

30–60ml/2–4 tbsp chopped flat leaf parsley, to taste

salt and ground black pepper

shaved Parmesan cheese, to serve

1 Heat the oil in a large pan. Add the pancetta, celery, carrots and onion and cook over a low heat for 5 minutes, stirring constantly, until the vegetables are softened.

2 Add the garlic and tomatoes, breaking them up with a wooden spoon. Pour in the stock. Season to taste and bring to the boil. Half cover the pan, lower the heat and simmer gently for 20 minutes, until the vegetables are soft.

3 Drain the beans and add to the pan with the macaroni. Bring to the boil again. Cover, lower the heat and continue to simmer for about 20 minutes more. Check the consistency and add more stock if necessary. Stir in the parsley and taste for seasoning.

4 Serve hot, sprinkled with plenty of Parmesan cheese.

Per portion Energy 198kcal/833kJ; Protein 15.6g; Carbohydrate 23.3g, of which sugars 3.9g; Fat 5.4g, of which saturates 1.4g; Cholesterol 30mg; Calcium 31mg; Fibre 3.2g; Sodium 224mg.

Summer minestrone

For the warmer months, this colourful and delicious light version of the classic soup is full of summer vegetables and herbs, with new potatoes replacing the pasta.

Serves 4

45ml/3 tbsp olive oil

1 large onion, finely chopped

15ml/1 tbsp sun-dried tomato paste

450g/1lb ripe Italian plum tomatoes, peeled and finely chopped

450g/1lb green and yellow courgettes (zucchini), trimmed and chopped

3 waxy new potatoes, diced

2 garlic cloves, crushed

1.2 litres/2 pints/5 cups chicken stock

60ml/4 tbsp shredded fresh basil

50g/2oz/⅔ cup grated Parmesan cheese

salt and ground black pepper

1 Heat the oil in a large pan, then add the chopped onion and cook gently for about 5 minutes, stirring constantly.

2 Stir in the sun-dried tomato paste, chopped tomatoes, chopped green and yellow courgettes, diced new potatoes and crushed garlic.

3 Mix together well and cook gently for 10 minutes, uncovered, shaking the pan frequently to stop the vegetables sticking to the base.

4 Carefully pour in the chicken stock. Bring to the boil, lower the heat, half cover the pan and simmer gently for 15 minutes or until the vegetables are just tender. Add more stock if necessary.

5 Remove the pan from the heat and stir in the basil and half the cheese. Taste for seasoning. Serve hot, sprinkled with the remaining cheese.

Per portion Energy 201kcal/839kJ; Protein 8.1g; Carbohydrate 18.1g, of which sugars 7.8g; Fat 11.2g, of which saturates 3.4g; Cholesterol 10mg; Calcium 170mg; Fibre 3g; Sodium 138mg.

Clam, mushroom and potato chowder

This one-pot dish is hearty and substantial enough for supper. The chowder includes sweet, delicately flavoured clams and the earthy flavours of wild and cultivated mushrooms.

Serves 4

48 clams, scrubbed

50g/2oz/¼ cup unsalted (sweet) butter

1 large onion, chopped

1 celery stick, sliced

1 carrot, sliced

225g/8oz assorted wild and cultivated mushrooms

225g/8oz floury potatoes, sliced

1.2 litres/2 pints/5 cups boiling light chicken or vegetable stock

1 thyme sprig

4 parsley stalks

salt and ground black pepper

thyme sprigs, to garnish

1 Place the clams in a large, heavy pan, discarding any that are open. Add 1cm/½in of water to the pan, then cover and bring to the boil.

2 Cook over a medium heat for 6–8 minutes, shaking the pan occasionally, until the clams open (discard any clams that do not open).

3 Drain the clams over a bowl and remove most of the shells, leaving some in the shells as a garnish.

4 Strain the cooking juices into the bowl, add all the cooked clams and set aside.

5 Add the butter, onion, celery and carrot to the pan and cook gently until softened but not coloured.

6 Add the assorted mushrooms and cook for 3–4 minutes until their juices begin to appear. Add the potato slices, the clams and their juices, the chicken or vegetable stock, thyme sprig and parsley stalks.

7 Bring the chowder to the boil, then reduce the heat, cover and simmer for about 25 minutes.

8 Season to taste with salt and pepper, ladle into individual soup bowls, and serve immediately, garnished with thyme sprigs.

Per portion Energy 203kcal/848kJ; Protein 10.8g; Carbohydrate 15.8g, of which sugars 5.2g; Fat 11.2g, of which saturates 6.8g; Cholesterol 60mg; Calcium 66mg; Fibre 2.4g; Sodium 696mg.

Fisherman's soup

Use whichever fish and shellfish you prefer for this tasty main-course soup, which is almost as substantial as a stew. Serve with slices of home-made crusty brown or soda bread.

Serves 6

25g/1oz/2 tbsp butter

1 onion, finely chopped

1 garlic clove, crushed or chopped

1 small red (bell) pepper, seeded and chopped

2.5ml/½ tsp sugar

a dash of Tabasco sauce

25g/1oz/¼ cup plain (all-purpose) flour

about 600ml/1 pint/2½ cups fish stock

450g/1lb ripe tomatoes, skinned and chopped, or 400g/14oz can chopped tomatoes

115g/4oz/1½ cups mushrooms, chopped

about 300ml/½ pint/1¼ cups milk

225g/8oz white fish, such as haddock or whiting, filleted and skinned, and cut into bitesize cubes

115g/4oz smoked haddock or cod, skinned, and cut into bitesize cubes

12–18 mussels, cleaned (optional)

salt and ground black pepper

chopped fresh parsley or chives, to garnish

1 Melt the butter in a large heavy pan and cook the chopped onion and crushed garlic gently in it until softened but not browned. Add the chopped red pepper. Season with salt and pepper, the sugar and Tabasco sauce. Sprinkle the flour over and cook gently for 2 minutes, stirring. Gradually stir in the stock and add the tomatoes, with their juices and the mushrooms.

2 Bring to the boil over medium heat, stir well, then reduce the heat and simmer until the vegetables are soft. Add the milk and bring back to the boil.

3 Add the fish to the pan and simmer for 3 minutes, then add the mussels, if using, and cook for another 3–4 minutes, or until the fish is just tender but not breaking up. Discard any mussels that remain closed. Adjust the consistency with a little extra fish stock or milk, if necessary. Check the seasoning and serve immediately, garnished with parsley or chives.

Per portion Energy 142kcal/597kJ; Protein 13.9g; Carbohydrate 10.7g, of which sugars 7.1g; Fat 5.2g, of which saturates 2.9g; Cholesterol 36mg; Calcium 84mg; Fibre 1.7g; Sodium 91mg.

Bacon and barley broth

Use a good-sized bacon hock to flavour this soup, which is thick with barley and lentils. Hearty peasant cooking makes this a nutritious and comforting soup.

Serves 6–8

1 bacon hock, about 900g/2lb

75g/3oz/¹⁄₃ cup pearl barley

75g/3oz/¹⁄₃ cup lentils

2 leeks, sliced, or onions, diced

4 carrots, diced

200g/7oz swede (rutabaga), diced

3 potatoes, diced

small bunch of herbs (thyme, parsley, bay leaf)

1 small cabbage, trimmed, quartered or sliced

salt and ground black pepper

chopped fresh parsley, to garnish

brown bread, to serve

Cook's tip Traditionally, the cabbage is simply trimmed and quartered, although it may be thinly sliced or shredded, if you prefer.

1 Soak the bacon in cold water overnight. Next morning, drain it and put it into a large pan with enough fresh cold water to cover it. Bring to the boil, skim off any scum that rises to the surface, and then add the barley and lentils. Bring back to the boil and simmer for about 15 minutes.

2 Add the vegetables to the pan with some black pepper and the herbs. Bring back to the boil, reduce the heat and simmer gently for 1¹⁄₂ hours, or until the meat is tender.

3 Lift the bacon hock from the pan with a slotted spoon. Remove the skin, then take the meat off the bones and break it into bitesize pieces. Return to the pan with the cabbage. Discard the herbs and cook for a little longer until the cabbage is cooked to your liking.

4 Adjust the seasoning and ladle into large serving bowls, garnish with parsley and serve with freshly baked brown bread.

Per portion Energy 306kcal/1284kJ; Protein 17.7g; Carbohydrate 33.5g, of which sugars 8.3g; Fat 12.1g, of which saturates 4.3g; Cholesterol 35mg; Calcium 74mg; Fibre 4.6g; Sodium 1.05g.

Lamb and vegetable broth

A contemporary version of the classic Irish mutton soup, this meaty broth includes lots of winter vegetables. It is very tasty served with chunks of Irish soda bread.

Serves 6

675g/1½lb neck of lamb (US shoulder or breast) on the bone

1 large onion

2 bay leaves

3 carrots, chopped

½ white turnip, diced

½ small white cabbage, shredded

2 large leeks, thinly sliced

15ml/1 tbsp tomato purée (paste)

30ml/2 tbsp chopped fresh parsley

salt and ground black pepper

1 Trim any excess fat from the meat. Chop the onion, and put the lamb and bay leaves in a large pan. Add 1.5 litres/2½ pints/6¼ cups water and bring to the boil. Skim the surface and then simmer for about 1½–2 hours. Remove the lamb on to a board and leave to cool until ready to handle.

2 Remove the meat from the bones and cut into small pieces. Discard the bones and return the meat to the broth. Add the vegetables, tomato purée and parsley, and season well. Simmer for another 30 minutes, until the vegetables are tender. Ladle into soup bowls and serve.

Per portion Energy 162kcal/675kJ; Protein 13.1g; Carbohydrate 8.5g, of which sugars 7g; Fat 8.6g, of which saturates 3.8g; Cholesterol 44mg; Calcium 42mg; Fibre 3g; Sodium 55mg.

Oxtail soup

Frugal country cooks utilize every part of an animal. Even the cheapest cuts respond well to slow cooking – oxtail becomes rich, dark and tender when slow cooked.

Serves 4–6

1 oxtail, cut into joints, total weight about 1.3kg/3lb

25g/1oz/2 tbsp butter

2 medium onions, chopped

2 medium carrots, chopped

2 celery sticks, sliced

1 bacon rasher (strip), chopped

2 litres/3½ pints/8 cups beef stock

1 bouquet garni

2 bay leaves

30ml/2 tbsp flour

squeeze of fresh lemon juice

60ml/4 tbsp port, sherry or Madeira

salt and ground black pepper

1 Wash and dry the pieces of oxtail, trimming off any excess fat. Melt the butter in a large pan, and when foaming, add the oxtail a few pieces at a time and brown them quickly on all sides. Lift the meat out on to a plate.

2 To the same pan, add the onions, carrots, celery and bacon. Cook over a medium heat for 5–10 minutes, stirring, until the vegetables are softened.

3 Return the oxtail to the pan and add the stock, bouquet garni, bay leaves and seasoning. Bring just to the boil and skim off any foam. Cover and simmer gently for about 3 hours or until the meat is so tender that it is falling away from the bones.

4 Strain the mixture, discarding the vegetables, bouquet garni and bay leaves, and leave to stand.

5 When the oxtail has cooled sufficiently to handle, pick all the meat off the bones and cut it into small pieces.

6 Skim off any fat that has risen to the surface of the stock, then transfer the stock into a large pan. Add the pieces of meat and reheat.

7 With a whisk, blend the flour with a little cold water to make a smooth paste. Stir in a little of the hot stock, then stir the mixture into the pan. Bring to the boil, stirring, until the soup thickens slightly. Reduce the heat and simmer gently for about 5 minutes.

8 Season with salt, pepper and lemon juice to taste. Just before serving, stir in the port, sherry or Madeira.

Per portion Energy 459kcal/1914kJ; Protein 45.4g; Carbohydrate 6.5g, of which sugars 2.6g; Fat 26.8g, of which saturates 11.8g; Cholesterol 176mg; Calcium 36mg; Fibre 0.7g; Sodium 403mg.

Beef and split pea broth

A restorative and nutritious meaty broth that will taste even more delicious when reheated, this hearty country soup will warm and comfort on a dark winter evening.

Serves 6–8

450–675g/1–1½lb rib steak, or other stewing beef on the bone

2 large onions

50g/2oz/¼ cup pearl barley

50g/2oz/¼ cup green split peas

3 large carrots, chopped

2 white turnips, peeled and chopped into dice

3 celery stalks, chopped

1 large or 2 medium leeks, thinly sliced and washed in cold water

sea salt and ground black pepper

chopped fresh parsley, to serve

1 Bone the meat and put the bones and half an onion, roughly sliced, into a large pan. Cover with cold water, season with salt and pepper, and bring to the boil. Skim if necessary, then simmer until needed.

2 Meanwhile, trim any fat or gristle from the meat and cut into small pieces. Chop the remaining onions finely with a sharp knife.

3 Drain the stock from the bones, make it up with water to 2 litres/3½ pints/ 9 cups, and return to the rinsed pan with the meat, onions, barley and split peas.

4 Season, bring to the boil, and skim if necessary. Reduce the heat, cover and simmer for about 30 minutes.

5 Add the carrots, turnip, celery and leeks to the pan and simmer for a further 1 hour, or until the meat is tender. Check the seasoning and adjust if necessary.

6 Serve the soup immediately in large individual warmed bowls, generously sprinkled with the chopped parsley.

Per portion Energy 167kcal/705kJ; Protein 16g; Carbohydrate 21.4g, of which sugars 7.8g; Fat 2.6g, of which saturates 0.8g; Cholesterol 34mg; Calcium 54mg; Fibre 3.6g; Sodium 58mg.

Field mushrooms stuffed with hazelnuts

Meaty field mushrooms filled with an aromatic mix of garlic and parley and topped with crunchy chopped hazelnuts make a delicious vegetarian appetizer or side dish.

Serves 4

2 garlic cloves

grated rind of 1 lemon

90ml/6 tbsp olive oil

8 large field (portabello) mushrooms

50g/2oz/½ cup hazelnuts, coarsely chopped

30ml/2 tbsp chopped fresh parsley

salt and ground black pepper

1 Crush the garlic cloves with a little salt. Place in a bowl and stir in the grated lemon rind and the olive oil. If time allows, leave to infuse (steep).

2 Preheat the oven to 200°C/400°F/ Gas 6. Arrange the field mushrooms, stalk side up, in a single layer in an ovenproof earthenware dish.

3 Drizzle over about 60ml/4 tbsp of the oil mixture and bake in the oven for about 10 minutes.

4 Remove the mushrooms from the oven and baste them with the remaining oil mixture, then sprinkle the chopped hazelnuts evenly over the top.

5 Bake for a further 10–15 minutes, or until the mushrooms are tender. Season with salt and pepper and sprinkle with chopped parsley. Serve immediately.

Cook's tip Almost any unsalted nuts can be used in place of the hazelnuts in this recipe – try pine nuts, cashew nuts, almonds or walnuts. Nuts can go rancid quickly so, for the freshest flavour, either buy nuts in small quantities or buy them in shells and remove the shells just before use.

Per portion Energy 255kcal/1052kJ; Protein 5.2g; Carbohydrate 1.7g, of which sugars 1g; Fat 25.4g, of which saturates 3.1g; Cholesterol 0mg; Calcium 43mg; Fibre 3.1g; Sodium 12mg.

Wild mushroom and sun-dried tomato soufflés

Foraged wild mushrooms would be ideal for this recipe. These delightful soufflés are remarkably easy to prepare, and are perfect either as an appetizer or light lunch.

Serves 4

25g/1oz/½ cup dried cep mushrooms

40g/1½oz/3 tbsp butter, plus extra for greasing

20ml/4 tsp grated Parmesan cheese

40g/1½oz/⅓ cup plain (all-purpose) flour

250ml/8fl oz/1 cup milk

50g/2oz/½ cup grated mature (sharp) Cheddar cheese

4 eggs, separated

2 sun-dried tomatoes in oil, drained and chopped

15ml/1 tbsp chopped fresh chives

salt and ground black pepper

Cook's tip A variety of different dried mushrooms are available – any can be used instead of the ceps.

1 Place the ceps in a bowl, pour over enough warm water to cover and leave to soak for 15 minutes. Grease four individual earthenware soufflé dishes with a little butter.

2 Sprinkle the grated Parmesan cheese into the soufflé dishes and rotate each dish to coat the sides with cheese. Preheat the oven to 190°C/375°F/Gas 5.

3 Melt the 40g/1½oz/3 tbsp of butter in a large pan, remove from the heat and stir in the flour. Cook over a low heat for 1 minute, stirring constantly. Remove the pan from the heat and gradually stir in the milk. Return to the heat and bring to the boil, stirring constantly, until the sauce has thickened.

4 Remove the sauce from the heat, then stir in the grated Cheddar cheese and plenty of seasoning. Beat in the egg yolks, one at a time, then stir in the chopped sun-dried tomatoes and the chives. Drain the soaked mushrooms, then coarsely chop them and add them to the cheese sauce.

5 Whisk the egg whites until they stand in soft peaks. Mix one spoonful into the sauce, then carefully fold in the remainder. Divide the mixture among the soufflé dishes and bake for 25 minutes, or until the soufflés are golden brown on top, well risen and just firm to the touch. Serve immediately – before they sink.

Per portion Energy 290kcal/1207kJ; Protein 14.7g; Carbohydrate 11.6g, of which sugars 3.9g; Fat 20.8g, of which saturates 11.2g; Cholesterol 232mg; Calcium 274mg; Fibre 0.6g; Sodium 305mg.

Gamekeeper's terrine

Hare and other furred game are popular in country cooking, having been hunted as food for centuries. For tender meat and a good flavour, use young hare that has been hung for at least a week. Rabbit would also be delicious in this terrine, or a mixture of minced pork and rabbit meat. Make sure you have plenty of hot toast to serve with it.

Serves 4–6

5 dried mushrooms, rinsed and soaked in warm water for 30 minutes

saddle, thighs, liver, heart and lungs of 1 hare

2 onions, cut into wedges

1 carrot, chopped

1 parsnip, chopped

4 bay leaves

10 allspice berries

300g/11oz calf's liver

165g/5½oz unsmoked streaky (fatty) bacon rashers (strips)

75g/3oz/1½ cups soft white breadcrumbs

4 eggs

105ml/7 tbsp 95 per cent proof Polish spirit or vodka

5ml/1 tsp freshly grated nutmeg

10ml/2 tsp dried marjoram

10g/¼oz juniper berries

4 garlic cloves, crushed

150g/5oz smoked streaky (fatty) bacon rashers (strips)

salt and ground black pepper, to taste

redcurrant jelly and salad, to serve

Cook's tip To make sure the bacon doesn't shrink during cooking, stretch each rasher (strip) out thinly on a board with the back of a knife.

1 Drain the mushrooms and slice into strips. Put the pieces of hare in a large pan and pour in enough water to just cover. Add the onions, carrot, parsnip, mushrooms, bay leaves and allspice.

2 Bring to the boil, then cover and simmer gently for 1 hour. Add a pinch of salt and allow the meat to cool in the stock.

3 Slice the liver and 50g/2oz unsmoked bacon into small pieces and put in a medium pan. Add a ladleful of the stock and simmer for 15 minutes.

4 Preheat the oven to 180°C/350°F/Gas 4. Put two ladlefuls of the stock in a small bowl, add the breadcrumbs and leave to soak.

5 Remove the hare pieces, liver and bacon from the stock and chop finely with a large knife.

6 Transfer to a large bowl, then add the soaked breadcrumbs, eggs, Polish spirit or vodka, nutmeg, marjoram, juniper berries and crushed garlic. Season to taste and mix well to combine thoroughly.

7 Line a 1.2 litre/2 pint/5 cup ovenproof dish with the smoked and remaining unsmoked bacon rashers, making sure they overhang the edges. Spoon in the meat mixture and bring the overhanging bacon over the top. Cover with buttered baking parchment, then cover with a lid or foil.

8 Place the dish in a roasting pan containing boiling water, then put in the oven and bake for 1½ hours, or until a skewer pushed into the centre comes out clean and the juices run clear. Remove the baking parchment and lid or foil about 15 minutes before the end of cooking to allow the terrine to brown.

9 Remove from the oven, and take the dish out of the roasting pan. Cover the terrine with baking parchment and a board and weight down with a 900g/2lb weight (such as two cans). Leave to cool, then turn out on to a serving dish. Serve in slices with redcurrant jelly and a green salad.

Per portion Energy 266kcal/1112kJ; Protein 27.1g; Carbohydrate 6.4g, of which sugars 1.4g; Fat 14g, of which saturates 5g; Cholesterol 182mg; Calcium 25mg; Fibre 0.3g; Sodium 432mg.

Fish and shellfish

Steamed, grilled or barbecued, fish and shellfish are the ultimate fast food. More elaborate dishes, such as Bouillabaisse, originate from the practical needs of fisher folk – after selling the prime catch, the leftover small or ugly fish would be included in tasty and filling stews, transforming them into delicious and nutritious meals. Many cultures share the same basic fish recipes, which can be adapted to include whichever fish are available.

Cod and bean casserole with saffron and paprika

It's sometimes nice to dine away from the table, and this is just the no-nonsense dish to do it with. With everything cooked in one pot, this appetizing casserole with chunks of fresh, flaky cod can be served simply with hunks of crusty bread and a crisp green side salad.

Serves 6–8

1 large red (bell) pepper

45ml/3 tbsp olive oil

4 rashers (strips) streaky (fatty) bacon, roughly chopped

4 garlic cloves, finely chopped

1 onion, sliced

10ml/2 tsp paprika

5ml/1 tsp hot pimentón (smoked Spanish paprika)

large pinch of saffron threads or 1 sachet powdered saffron, soaked in 45ml/3 tbsp hot water

400g/14oz jar Spanish butter (lima) beans (judias del barco or judias blancas guisadas) or canned haricot (navy) beans, drained and rinsed

about 600ml/1 pint/2½ cups fish stock, or water and 60ml/4 tbsp Thai fish sauce

6 plum tomatoes, quartered

350g/12oz fresh skinned cod fillet, cut into large chunks

45ml/3 tbsp chopped fresh coriander (cilantro), plus a few sprigs to garnish

salt and ground black pepper

crusty bread, to serve

1 Preheat the grill (broiler) and line the pan with foil. Halve the red pepper and scoop out the seeds.

2 Place the red pepper, cut-side down, in the grill pan and grill (broil) under a hot heat for about 10–15 minutes, until the skin is black and charred.

3 Put the pepper into a plastic bag, seal and leave for 10 minutes to steam, which will make the skin easier to remove.

4 Remove the pepper from the bag, peel and chop into large pieces.

5 Heat the olive oil in a pan, then add the chopped streaky bacon and the chopped garlic. Fry for about 2 minutes, then add the sliced onion.

6 Cover the pan and cook for about another 5 minutes until the onion is soft. Stir in the paprika and pimentón, the saffron and its soaking water, and salt and pepper.

7 Stir the beans into the pan and add just enough of the stock to cover them. Bring to the boil and simmer, uncovered, for about 15 minutes, stirring occasionally to prevent it from sticking.

8 Stir in the chopped pepper and tomato quarters. Drop in the cubes of cod and bury them in the sauce.

9 Cover and simmer for 5 minutes until the fish is cooked. Stir in the chopped coriander.

10 Divide the stew equally between six to eight warmed soup plates or bowls, garnishing each one with the coriander sprigs. Serve with lots of crusty bread.

Cook's tip If you prefer to use dried beans, soak them in water for 12 hours or overnight, rinse and then boil for 40–50 minutes depending on the beans.

Per portion Energy 449kcal/1883kJ; Protein 44.5g; Carbohydrate 25.3g, of which sugars 3.9g; Fat 19.5g, of which saturates 3g; Cholesterol 84mg; Calcium 85mg; Fibre 9.8g; Sodium 403mg.

Salt cod fritters with garlic aioli

A favourite dish of Portuguese, Spanish and French fishermen, salt cod fritters are delicious when served with an aromatic garlic mayonnaise. If you have any leftover aioli, it can be stirred into a bowl of cold potatoes to make a delicious potato salad.

Serves 6

450g/1lb salt cod

500g/1¼lb floury potatoes

300ml/½ pint/1¼ cups milk

6 spring onions (scallions), finely chopped

30ml/2 tbsp extra virgin olive oil

30ml/2 tbsp chopped fresh parsley

juice of ½ lemon, to taste

2 eggs, beaten

60ml/4 tbsp plain (all-purpose) flour

90g/3½oz/1⅓ cups dry white breadcrumbs

vegetable oil, for shallow frying

salt and ground black pepper

lemon wedges and salad, to serve

For the aioli

2 large garlic cloves

2 egg yolks

300ml/½ pint/1¼ cups olive oil

lemon juice, to taste

1 Soak the salt cod in cold water for 24 hours, changing the water about 5 times. The cod should swell as it rehydrates and a tiny piece should not taste too salty when tried. Drain well.

2 Cook the potatoes, unpeeled, in a pan of boiling salted water for about 20 minutes, until tender. Drain, then peel and mash the potatoes.

3 Poach the cod very gently in the milk with half the spring onions for 10–15 minutes, or until it flakes easily. Remove the cod and flake it with a fork into a bowl, discarding bones and skin.

4 Add 60ml/4 tbsp mashed potato to the flaked cod and beat with a wooden spoon. Work in the olive oil, then gradually add the remaining potato. Beat in the remaining spring onions and parsley. Season with lemon juice and pepper to taste – it may need a little salt. Beat in 1 egg, then chill until firm.

5 Shape the mixture into 12 round cakes. Coat them in flour, then dip in the remaining egg and coat with the breadcrumbs. Chill until ready to fry.

6 Meanwhile, make the aioli. Place the garlic and a good pinch of salt in a mortar and pound to a paste with a pestle. Using a small whisk or a wooden spoon, gradually work in the egg yolks.

7 Add the olive oil, a drop at a time, until half is incorporated. When the sauce is as thick as soft butter, beat in 5–10ml/ 1–2 tsp lemon juice, then continue adding oil until the aioli is very thick. Adjust the seasoning, adding lemon juice to taste.

8 Heat 2cm/¾in depth of oil in a frying pan. Add the fritters and cook over a medium-high heat for 4 minutes. Turn over and cook for a further 4 minutes on the other side, until crisp and golden. Drain on kitchen paper, then serve with the aioli, lemon wedges and salad leaves.

Per portion Energy 653kcal/2721kJ; Protein 32.7g; Carbohydrate 28.1g, of which sugars 4.2g; Fat 46.4g, of which saturates 7.6g; Cholesterol 178mg; Calcium 123mg; Fibre 1.4g; Sodium 472mg.

Whole baked salmon with watercress sauce

Served as an impressive centrepiece, this whole baked salmon would make a stunning focal point for a country dining table. Healthy and delicious, the dish is equally good served hot or cold. The peppery watercress sauce and fresh cucumber complement the salmon perfectly.

Serves 6–8

2–3kg/4½–6½lb salmon, cleaned, with head and tail left on

3–5 spring onions (scallions), thinly sliced

1 lemon, thinly sliced

1 cucumber, thinly sliced

salt and ground black pepper

sprigs of fresh dill, to garnish

lemon wedges, to serve

For the sauce

3 garlic cloves, chopped

200g/7oz watercress leaves, finely chopped

40g/1½oz/¾ cup finely chopped fresh tarragon

300g/11oz/1¼ cups mayonnaise

15–30ml/1–2 tbsp lemon juice

200g/7oz/scant 1 cup unsalted (sweet) butter

1 Preheat the oven to 180°C/350°F/ Gas 4. Rinse the salmon and lay it on a large piece of foil. Stuff the fish with the sliced spring onions and lemon. Season with salt and black pepper.

2 Loosely fold the foil around the fish and fold the edges over to seal. Bake in the preheated oven for about 1 hour.

3 Remove the fish from the oven and leave it to stand, still wrapped in the foil, for about 15 minutes. Then gently unwrap the foil parcel and set the salmon aside to cool.

4 When the fish has cooled, carefully lift it on to a large plate, still covered with lemon slices. Cover the fish tightly with clear film (plastic wrap) and chill for several hours in the refrigerator.

5 Remove the lemon slices from the top of the fish. Use a blunt knife to lift up the edge of the skin and carefully peel the skin away from the flesh, avoiding tearing the flesh. Pull out any fins at the same time. Carefully turn the salmon over and repeat on the other side. Leave the head on for serving, if you wish. Discard the skin.

Variation If you prefer to poach the fish rather than baking it, you will need to use a fish kettle. Place the salmon on the rack in the kettle. Cover the salmon completely with cold water, place the lid over to cover, and slowly bring to a simmer. Cook for 5–10 minutes per 450g/1lb until tender. The fish is cooked when pink and opaque.

6 To make the sauce, put the garlic, watercress, tarragon, mayonnaise and lemon juice in a food processor or bowl, and process or mix to combine.

7 Melt the butter, then add to the watercress mixture a little at a time, processing or stirring until the butter has been incorporated and the sauce is thick and smooth. Cover and chill.

8 Arrange the cucumber slices in overlapping rows along the length of the fish, so that they look like large fish scales. You can also slice the cucumber diagonally to produce longer slices for decoration. Trim the edges with scissors. Serve the fish, garnished with dill and lemon wedges, with the watercress sauce alongside.

Cook's tip Do not prepare the sauce hours before you need it because the watercress will discolour. Alternatively, add the watercress just before serving.

Per portion Energy 1044kcal/4323kJ; Protein 51.6g; Carbohydrate 1.4g, of which sugars 1.2g; Fat 92.4g, of which saturates 28.5g; Cholesterol 231mg; Calcium 135mg; Fibre 0.7g; Sodium 558mg.

Maryland crab cakes with tartare sauce

One of the most famous American country dishes, these crab cakes are a modern version of Baltimore crab cakes. The tasty white crab meat is coated in breadcrumbs and fried.

Serves 4

675g/1½lb fresh crab meat

1 egg, beaten

30ml/2 tbsp mayonnaise

15ml/1 tbsp Worcestershire sauce

15ml/1 tbsp sherry

30ml/2 tbsp finely chopped
fresh parsley

15ml/1 tbsp finely chopped
fresh chives

salt and ground black pepper

45ml/3 tbsp olive oil

For the sauce

1 egg yolk

15ml/1 tbsp white wine vinegar

30ml/2 tbsp Dijon-style mustard

250ml/8fl oz/1 cup vegetable oil

30ml/2 tbsp fresh lemon juice

20g/¾oz/¼ cup finely chopped
spring onions (scallions)

30ml/2 tbsp chopped drained capers

few finely chopped sour dill pickles

60ml/4 tbsp finely chopped
fresh parsley

1 Pick over the crab meat, removing any shell or cartilage.

2 In a mixing bowl, combine the beaten egg with the mayonnaise, Worcestershire sauce, sherry and herbs. Season with salt and pepper. Gently fold in the crab meat. Divide the mixture into eight portions and gently form each one into an oval cake. Place on a baking sheet between layers of baking parchment and chill for 1 hour.

3 Make the sauce. In a bowl, beat the egg yolk. Add the vinegar, mustard and salt and pepper, and whisk for 10 seconds. Whisk in the oil in a slow, steady stream.

4 Add the lemon juice, spring onions, capers, pickles and parsley and mix well. Check the seasoning. Cover and chill for at least 30 minutes.

5 Preheat the grill (broiler). Brush the crab cakes with the olive oil. Place on an oiled baking sheet, in one layer.

6 Grill (broil) 15cm/6in from the heat until golden brown, about 5 minutes on each side. Serve the crab cakes hot with the tartare sauce.

Variation You can use defrosted frozen or canned crab meat instead.

Per portion Energy 710kcal/2934kJ; Protein 33.8g; Carbohydrate 1.9g, of which sugars 1.7g; Fat 62.6g, of which saturates 8.1g; Cholesterol 225mg; Calcium 234mg; Fibre 0.2g; Sodium 1249mg.

Prawn, chilli and potato stew

This quick and tasty shellfish stew makes the most of new potatoes that have plenty of flavour, such as Jersey Royals, Maris Piper or Nicola. You could add extra chilli if you prefer the dish really hot, then serve with a garden salad and crusty bread to mop up the sauce.

Serves 4

675g/1½lb small new potatoes, scrubbed

15g/½oz/½ cup fresh coriander (cilantro)

350g/12oz jar tomato and chilli sauce

300g/11oz cooked peeled prawns (shrimp), thawed and drained if frozen

1 Cook the potatoes in lightly salted, boiling water for 15 minutes, until tender. Drain and return to the pan.

2 Finely chop half the coriander and add to the pan with the tomato and chilli sauce and 90ml/6 tbsp water. Bring to the boil, reduce the heat, cover and allow to simmer gently for 5 minutes.

3 Stir in the prawns and heat until they are warmed through. Do not overheat the prawns or they will quickly shrivel, becoming tough and tasteless. Spoon into bowls and serve sprinkled with the remaining coriander, torn into pieces.

Per portion Energy 218kcal/924kJ; Protein 16.9g; Carbohydrate 30.4g, of which sugars 5.4g; Fat 4.1g, of which saturates 0.7g; Cholesterol 146mg; Calcium 84mg; Fibre 2.9g; Sodium 171mg.

Spaghetti vongole

One of Italy's most famous country recipes, this tasty dish using carpet shell clams is an effortlessly easy supper or lunch dish that can be made with any small clams. It is lovely served with a green salad of peppery rocket or watercress leaves.

Serves 4

1kg/2¼lb fresh clams

60ml/4 tbsp olive oil

45ml/3 tbsp chopped fresh flat leaf parsley

120ml/4fl oz/½ cup dry white wine

350g/12oz dried spaghetti

2 garlic cloves

salt and ground black pepper

1 Scrub the clams under cold running water, discarding any that are open or that do not close when sharply tapped against the work surface.

2 Heat half the oil in a large pan, add the clams and 15ml/1 tbsp of the parsley and cook over a high heat for a few seconds.

3 Pour in the wine, then cover tightly. Cook for 5 minutes, shaking the pan frequently, until the clams have opened. Meanwhile, cook the pasta in salted boiling water according to the instructions on the packet.

4 Using a slotted spoon, transfer the clams to a bowl, discarding any that have failed to open.

5 Strain the liquid and set it aside. Put eight clams in their shells to one side for the garnish, then remove the rest from their shells.

6 Heat the remaining oil in the clean pan. Fry the garlic cloves until golden, crushing them with the back of a spoon. Remove the garlic with a slotted spoon and discard.

7 Add the shelled clams to the oil remaining in the pan, gradually add some of the strained liquid from the clams, then add plenty of pepper.

8 Cook for about 1–2 minutes, gradually adding a little more liquid as the sauce reduces. Add the remaining parsley and cook for a further 1–2 minutes.

9 Drain the pasta, add it to the pan and toss well. Serve in individual dishes, carefully scooping the shelled clams from the bottom of the pan and placing some of them on top of each serving.

10 Garnish with the reserved clams in their shells and serve immediately.

Per portion Energy 519kcal/2187kJ; Protein 30.9g; Carbohydrate 67.7g, of which sugars 3.4g; Fat 13.5g, of which saturates 2g; Cholesterol 84mg; Calcium 142mg; Fibre 3.2g; Sodium 1508mg.

Seafood pie

A taste of the sea, a good fish pie includes both fresh and smoked fish – ideal winter fare when the fishing fleets are hampered by gales and fresh fish is in short supply. Add shellfish such as mussels, and a few capers and dill for extra piquancy.

Serves 4–5

450g/1lb haddock or cod fillet

225g/8oz smoked haddock or cod

150ml/¼ pint/⅔ cup milk

150ml/¼ pint/⅔ cup water

1 slice of lemon

1 small bay leaf

a few fresh parsley stalks

For the sauce

25g/1oz/2 tbsp butter

25g/1oz/¼ cup plain (all-purpose) flour

5ml/1 tbsp lemon juice, or to taste

45ml/3 tbsp chopped fresh parsley

ground black pepper

For the topping

450g/1lb potatoes, boiled and mashed

25g/1oz/2 tbsp butter

1 Preheat the oven to 190°C/375°F/ Gas 5. Rinse the fish, cut it into manageable pieces and put into a pan with the milk, water, lemon, bay leaf and parsley stalks.

2 Bring the fish slowly to the boil, then simmer gently for 15 minutes until tender. Strain and reserve 300ml/ ½ pint/1¼ cups of the cooking liquor. Leave the fish until cool, then flake the cooked flesh and discard the skin and bones. Set aside.

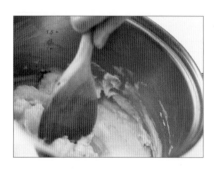

3 To make the sauce, melt the butter in a heavy pan, add the flour and cook for 1–2 minutes over low heat, stirring constantly.

4 Gradually add the reserved cooking liquor, stirring well to make a smooth sauce.

Variations
• Almost any mixture of prepared seafood can go into this fish pie. Cut all the fish into roughly the same size, and cut large scallops or prawns in half.
• Try adding other soft herbs such as chervil, dill or chives to the sauce, or a teaspoon of grain mustard.

5 Simmer the sauce gently for about 1–2 minutes, then remove the pan from the heat and stir in the flaked fish, chopped parsley and lemon juice. Season to taste with ground black pepper.

6 Turn into a buttered 1.75 litre/3 pint/ 7½ cup pie dish or shallow casserole, cover evenly with the mashed potato for the topping, smoothing with the back of a fork if necessary. Cut the butter into small pieces and dot the potato with the butter.

7 Cook the pie in the preheated oven for about 20 minutes, or until it is thoroughly heated through. The potato topping should be golden brown and crunchy.

8 Divide the pie among four or five warmed plates and serve immediately with a lightly cooked green vegetable, such as fresh broccoli florets.

Per portion Energy 336kcal/1413kJ; Protein 35.1g; Carbohydrate 24.3g, of which sugars 0.9g; Fat 11.6g, of which saturates 6.7g; Cholesterol 87mg; Calcium 45mg; Fibre 1.7g; Sodium 587mg.

Poultry and game

Chicken and other poultry are among the most popular and versatile meats, and they can be prepared in a huge variety of ways, from a simple roasted bird to delicious slow-cooked classics such as Coq au Vin. In the past, game was a seasonal meat available only at certain times of the year, but it is now possible to obtain a wide variety of game all year round. It is, however, still rewarding to cook game with traditional seasonal ingredients.

Roast chicken with herb stuffing

A staple of traditional country cooking, a simply roasted free-range chicken with herbs and home-made stuffing is hard to beat. Serve with roast potatoes, sausages, bacon rolls and seasonal vegetables, along with a fruit jelly such as cranberry sauce or elderberry jelly.

Serves 6

1 large chicken, about 1.8kg/4lb, with giblets and neck if possible

1 small onion, sliced

1 small carrot, sliced

small bunch of parsley and thyme

15g/½oz/1 tbsp butter

30ml/2 tbsp chicken fat or oil

6 rashers (strips) of streaky (fatty) bacon

salt and ground black pepper

For the stuffing

1 onion, finely chopped

50g/2oz/¼ cup butter

150g/5oz/2½ cups fresh white breadcrumbs

15ml/1 tbsp fresh chopped parsley

15ml/1 tbsp fresh chopped mixed herbs, such as thyme, marjoram and chives

finely grated rind and juice of ½ lemon

1 small egg, lightly beaten (optional)

15ml/1 tbsp plain (all-purpose) flour

1 Remove the giblets from the chicken; also remove the piece of fat which is found just inside the vent and put this fat into a roasting pan – it can be rendered down and used when cooking the roast potatoes. Wipe out the inside of the bird thoroughly. Separate the liver from the rest of the giblets, chop it and set it aside to use in the gravy.

2 Put the giblets and the neck into a pan with the sliced onion and sliced carrot, the bunch of parsley and thyme and a good sprinkling of salt and pepper. Add enough cold water to cover generously, bring to the boil and leave to simmer gently for about 1 hour. Strain the chicken stock and discard the giblets. Preheat the oven to 200°C/400°F/Gas 6.

3 Meanwhile, make the herb stuffing: cook the chopped onion in the butter in a large pan over a low heat without colouring for a few minutes until it is just beginning to soften.

4 Remove from the heat, and add the breadcrumbs, fresh herbs and grated lemon rind. Mix thoroughly. Mix in the lemon juice, beaten egg, if using, and salt and pepper. (The egg will bind the stuffing and make it firmer when cooked, but it can be omitted if you prefer a lighter, more crumbly texture.)

5 Spoon the stuffing into the neck cavity of the chicken, without packing it in too tightly, and secure the opening with a small skewer. Spread the breast with the butter, then put the chicken fat or oil into a roasting pan and lay the bird in it. Season and lay the bacon rashers over the top of the bird to protect it in the oven.

6 Weigh the stuffed chicken and work out the cooking time at 20 minutes per 450g/1lb and 20 minutes over, then put into the preheated oven. After 20 minutes, reduce the temperature to 180°C/350°F/Gas 4 for another 45–60 minutes, or until cooked. Test by inserting a sharp knife between the body and thigh: if the juices run clear with no hint of blood, it is cooked.

7 Transfer the cooked chicken to a serving dish and allow it to rest for 10 minutes while you make the gravy.

8 To make the gravy, pour off the excess fat from the roasting pan, then add the finely chopped liver and stir over low heat for 1 minute, or until it has turned light brown. Sprinkle in just enough flour to absorb the remaining chicken fat and cook gently, stirring to blend, for 1 or 2 minutes. Gradually add some of the giblet stock, scraping the pan to dissolve the residues and stirring well to make a smooth gravy.

9 Bring to the boil, stirring, gradually adding more stock until the consistency is as you like it. Adjust the seasoning, and then pour into a heated sauceboat to hand round separately.

10 Carve the chicken. Serve on heated plates with the herb stuffing and gravy.

Per portion Energy 562kcal/2342kJ; Protein 40.9g; Carbohydrate 23.2g, of which sugars 2.7g; Fat 34.5g, of which saturates 11.9g; Cholesterol 216mg; Calcium 72mg; Fibre 1.5g; Sodium 381mg.

Lemon and garlic pot roast chicken

Pot roasting is at the heart of rustic cooking. Easy to prepare and slow cooked, this is a great family dish. Serve with baked rice, mashed potatoes or thick bread.

Serves 4

30ml/2 tbsp olive oil

25g/1oz/2 tbsp butter

175g/6oz/1 cup smoked lardons, or roughly chopped streaky (fatty) bacon

8 garlic cloves, peeled

4 onions, quartered

10ml/2 tsp plain (all-purpose) flour

600ml/1 pint/2½ cups chicken stock

2 lemons, thickly sliced

45ml/3 tbsp chopped fresh thyme

1 chicken, about 1.3–1.6kg/3–3½lb

2 x 400g/14oz cans flageolet, cannellini or haricot (navy) beans, drained and rinsed

salt and ground black pepper

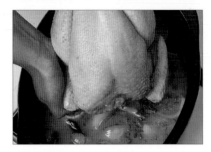

3 Bring to the boil, stirring constantly until thickened, then place the chicken on top. Season well. Transfer the casserole to the oven. Cook for 1 hour, basting the chicken once or twice during cooking to ensure it stays moist.

4 Baste the chicken again. Stir the beans into the casserole and return it to the oven for a further 30 minutes, or until the chicken is cooked through and tender. Carve the chicken into thick slices and serve with the beans.

1 Preheat the oven to 190°C/375°F/ Gas 5. Heat the oil and butter in a flameproof casserole that is large enough to hold the chicken with a little room around the sides. Add the lardons and cook until golden. Remove with a slotted spoon and drain on kitchen paper.

2 Add the garlic and onions and brown over a high heat. Stir in the flour, then the stock. Return the lardons to the pan with the lemon, thyme and seasoning.

Per portion Energy 887kcal/3696kJ; Protein 62.5g; Carbohydrate 45.5g, of which sugars 12.9g; Fat 51.7g, of which saturates 16g; Cholesterol 256mg; Calcium 187mg; Fibre 13.9g; Sodium 1519mg.

Chicken baked with forty cloves of garlic

Don't be put off by the amount of garlic in this traditional dish. The garlic heads become soft, sweet and fragrant when cooked, and impart a mouth-watering aroma.

Serves 4–5

5–6 whole heads of garlic

15g/½oz/1 tbsp butter

45ml/3 tbsp olive oil

1.8–2kg/4–4½lb chicken

150g/5oz/1¼ cups plain (all-purpose) flour, plus 5ml/1 tsp

75ml/5 tbsp white port, Pineau de Charentes or other white, fortified wine

2–3 fresh tarragon or rosemary sprigs

30ml/2 tbsp crème fraîche

few drops of lemon juice

salt and ground black pepper

1 Separate three of the heads of garlic into cloves and peel. Remove the first layer of papery skin from the remaining heads of garlic and leave whole. Preheat the oven to 180°C/350°F/Gas 4.

2 Heat the butter and 15ml/1 tbsp of the olive oil in a flameproof casserole that is just large enough to take the chicken and garlic. Add the chicken and cook over a medium heat, turning frequently, for 10 minutes, until it is browned all over. Sprinkle in 5ml/1 tsp flour and cook for 1 minute. Add the port or wine. Tuck in the whole heads of garlic and the peeled cloves with the herb sprigs.

3 Pour the remaining oil over the chicken and season to taste with salt and pepper. Rub all over to coat.

4 Mix the main batch of flour with enough water to make a firm dough. Roll it out into a long sausage and press around the rim of the casserole, then press on the lid, folding the dough up and over it to create a tight seal. Cook in the oven for 1½ hours.

5 To serve, lift off the lid to break the seal and remove the chicken and whole garlic to a serving platter and keep warm. Remove and discard the herb sprigs, then place the casserole on the hob and whisk to combine the garlic cloves with the juices. Add the crème fraîche and a little lemon juice to taste. Process the sauce in a food processor or blender if a smoother result is required. Serve the garlic purée with the chicken.

Per portion Energy 787kcal/3276kJ; Protein 51.3g; Carbohydrate 33.2g, of which sugars 1g; Fat 50.6g, of which saturates 14.5g; Cholesterol 248mg; Calcium 77mg; Fibre 2.2g; Sodium 212mg.

Puff pastry chicken pies

These versatile little pies can be filled with different kinds of meat. Although chicken is the most popular, they are also good with a mixture of game and chicken, or with fish or shellfish. They make a tempting afternoon snack, or you could have two or three of them, either hot or cold, with a refreshing salad for a delicious light lunch.

Makes about 12

1 chicken, weighing 1.6–2kg/3½–4½lb

45ml/3 tbsp olive oil

1 sausage, weighing about 250g/9oz

150g/5oz bacon

1 garlic clove

10 black peppercorns

1 onion stuck with 2 cloves

1 bunch of parsley, chopped

4 thyme or marjoram sprigs

juice of 1 lemon or 60ml/4 tbsp white wine vinegar

butter, for greasing

500g/1¼lb puff pastry, thawed if frozen

plain (all-purpose) flour, for dusting

2 egg yolks, lightly beaten

salt

1 Cut the chicken into pieces. Heat the oil in a large, heavy pan. Add the chicken pieces and cook over a medium-low heat, turning occasionally, for about 10 minutes, until golden brown on all sides.

2 Add the sausage, bacon, garlic, peppercorns, onion, parsley, thyme and lemon juice or vinegar. Pour in enough water to cover and bring to the boil. Lower the heat, cover and simmer for 1–1½ hours, until tender.

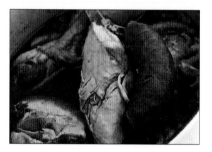

3 Remove all the meat from the stock with a slotted spoon. Then return the stock to the heat and cook, uncovered, until slightly reduced. Strain the stock into a bowl and season with salt to taste.

4 Remove and discard the chicken skin and bones and cut the meat into small pieces. Cut the sausage and bacon into small pieces. Mix all the meat together. Preheat the oven to 200°C/400°F/Gas 6. Grease a 12-cup muffin tin (pan) with butter.

5 Roll out the pastry thinly on a lightly floured surface and stamp out 12 rounds with a 7.5cm/3in cutter.

6 Gather the trimmings together and roll out thinly again, then stamp out 12 rounds with a 6cm/2½in cutter. Place the larger rounds in the cups of the prepared tin, pressing the pastry to the side with your thumb, and divide the meat among them.

7 Spoon in a little of the stock, then brush the edges with beaten egg yolk and cover with the smaller rounds, pinching the edges to seal.

8 Brush the remaining egg yolk over the top to glaze and make a small hole in the centre of each pie with a wooden cocktail stick (toothpick).

9 Bake for 15–25 minutes, until golden brown. Remove from the oven and leave to cool before serving.

Variation You can use the following dough as an alternative to puff pastry. Sift 500g/1¼lb/5 cups plain (all-purpose) flour into a bowl and make a well in the centre. Add 5 eggs and about 150g/5oz/⅔ cup of the leftover chicken fat to the well and mix together, adding some stock if necessary. Blend well, then shape the dough into a ball and leave to rest, wrapped in clear film (plastic wrap), for 30 minutes before rolling out.

Per pie Energy 368kcal/1534kJ; Protein 24.5g; Carbohydrate 18.3g, of which sugars 1.2g; Fat 22.8g, of which saturates 4.3g; Cholesterol 109mg; Calcium 44mg; Fibre 0.2g; Sodium 547mg.

Classic roast turkey with country stuffing

Traditionally served at Christmas or Thanksgiving, roast turkey is a splendid celebration dish. The rich herb stuffing in this recipe is made with calf's liver, but lamb's liver would be fine, too. Serve with cranberry jelly, which will taste even better if you make it yourself.

Serves 6

1 turkey, about 4.5–5.5kg/10–12lb, washed and patted dry with kitchen paper

25g/1oz/2 tbsp butter, melted

salt and ground black pepper, to taste

cranberry jelly, to serve

For the stuffing

200g/7oz/3½ cups fresh white breadcrumbs

175ml/6fl oz/¾ cup milk

25g/1oz/2 tbsp butter

1 egg, separated

1 calf's liver, about 600g/1lb 6oz, finely chopped

2 onions, finely chopped

90ml/6 tbsp chopped fresh dill

10ml/2 tsp clear honey

salt and ground black pepper, to taste

1 To make the stuffing, put the breadcrumbs and milk in a large bowl and soak until swollen and soft.

2 Melt the butter in a frying pan and mix 5ml/1 tsp with the egg yolk.

3 Heat the remaining butter in a frying pan and add the finely chopped calf's liver and onions. Fry gently for 5 minutes, until the onions are golden brown. Remove from the heat and leave to cool.

4 Preheat the oven to 180°C/350°F/ Gas 4. Add the cooled liver mixture to the soaked breadcrumbs and milk, then add the butter and egg yolk mixture, with the chopped dill, clear honey and seasoning.

5 In a clean bowl, whisk the egg white to soft peaks, then fold into the stuffing mixture, stirring gently to combine thoroughly.

6 Season the turkey inside and out with salt and pepper. Stuff the cavity with the stuffing mixture, then weigh to calculate the cooking time. Allow 20 minutes per 500g/1¼lb, plus an additional 20 minutes. Tuck the legs of the turkey inside the cavity and tie the end shut with string. Brush the outside with melted butter and transfer to a roasting pan. Place in the oven and roast for the calculated time.

7 Baste the turkey regularly during cooking, and cover with foil for the final 30 minutes if the skin becomes too brown. To test whether the turkey is cooked, pierce the thickest part of the thigh with a knife; the juices should run clear.

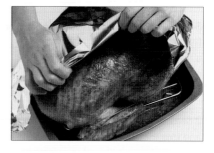

8 Remove the turkey from the oven, cover with foil and leave to rest for about 15 minutes. Carve into thin slices, then spoon over the juices and serve with the stuffing and cranberry jelly.

Per portion Energy 740kcal/3126kJ; Protein 112.3g; Carbohydrate 35.9g, of which sugars 7.3g; Fat 13.5g, of which saturates 6.6g; Cholesterol 507mg; Calcium 122mg; Fibre 1.7g; Sodium 517mg.

Raised game pie

The perfect picnic food traditionally taken on country shoots, this stylish dish makes a spectacular centrepiece when baked in a fluted raised pie mould. The hot water crust pastry is very easy to make, and the pie can be served with piccalilli and pickled onions.

Serves 10

25g/1oz/2 tbsp butter

1 onion, finely chopped

2 garlic cloves, finely chopped

900g/2lb mixed boneless game meat, such as skinless pheasant and/or pigeon breast, venison and rabbit, diced

30ml/2 tbsp chopped mixed fresh herbs such as parsley, thyme and marjoram

salt and ground black pepper

For the pâté

50g/2oz/¼ cup butter

2 garlic cloves, finely chopped

450g/1lb chicken livers, rinsed, trimmed and chopped

60ml/4 tbsp brandy

5ml/1 tsp ground mace

For the hot water crust pastry

675g/1½lb/6 cups strong plain (all-purpose) flour

5ml/1 tsp salt

115ml/3½fl oz/scant ½ cup milk

115ml/3½fl oz/scant ½ cup water

115g/4oz/½ cup lard, diced

115g/4oz/½ cup butter, diced

beaten egg, to glaze

For the jelly

300ml/½ pint/1¼ cups game or beef consommé

2.5ml/½ tsp powdered gelatine

1 Melt the butter in a small pan until foaming, then add the onion and garlic, and cook until softened but not coloured. Remove from the heat and mix with the diced game meat and the chopped mixed herbs. Season well, cover and chill.

2 To make the pâté, melt the butter in a pan until foaming. Add the garlic and chicken livers and cook until the livers are just browned. Remove the pan from the heat and stir in the brandy and mace. Purée the mixture in a blender or food processor until smooth, then set aside and leave to cool.

3 To make the pastry, sift the flour and salt into a bowl and make a well in the centre. Place the milk and water in a pan. Add the lard and butter and heat gently until melted, then bring to the boil and remove from the heat as soon as the mixture begins to bubble. Pour the hot liquid into the well in the flour and beat until smooth. Cover and leave until cool enough to handle.

4 Preheat the oven to 200°C/400°F/ Gas 6. Roll out two-thirds of the pastry and use to line a 23cm/9in raised pie mould. Spoon in half the game mixture and press it down evenly. Add the pâté, then top with the remaining game.

5 Roll out the remaining pastry to form a lid. Brush the edge of the pastry lining the mould with water and cover the pie with the lid. Trim off any excess. Pinch the edges together to seal. Make two holes in the centre of the lid and glaze with egg. Use pastry trimmings to roll out leaves to garnish the pie. Brush with egg.

6 Bake the pie for 20 minutes, cover with foil and cook for a further 10 minutes. Reduce the oven temperature to 150°C/300°F/Gas 2. Glaze the pie again with beaten egg and cook for a further 1½ hours, keeping the top covered loosely with foil.

7 Remove the pie from the oven and leave to stand for 15 minutes. Increase the oven temperature to 200°C/400°F/ Gas 6. Stand the mould on a baking sheet and remove the sides. Glaze the sides of the pie with beaten egg and cover the top with foil, then cook for a final 15 minutes to brown the sides. Cool completely, then chill the pie overnight.

8 For the jelly, heat the game or beef consommé in a small pan until just starting to bubble, whisk in the gelatine until dissolved and leave to cool until just setting. Using a small funnel, carefully pour the jellied consommé into the holes in the pie. Chill. This pie will keep in the refrigerator for up to 3 days.

Per portion Energy 731kcal/3058kJ; Protein 44g; Carbohydrate 54.3g, of which sugars 2.5g; Fat 32g, of which saturates 17.9g; Cholesterol 223mg; Calcium 163mg; Fibre 2.3g; Sodium 444mg.

Meat dishes

Freshly baked pies, slow-cooked pot roasts and flavoursome casseroles sum up all that is best in country cooking. From simple Sunday roasts to comfort food such as Shepherd's Pie and Lancashire Hotpot, there is a meat dish for every occasion in this chapter. Many of the recipes use economic cuts of meat and seasonal vegetables, so you can really make the most of the revival in home cooking.

Roast loin of pork with apple and spinach

Pork and apple are a well-loved combination, and loin of pork is a prime roasting joint. In this recipe the pork is stuffed with apples, but these could be replaced with apricots or prunes.

Serves 6–8

1.6–1.8kg/3½–4lb loin of pork, boned and skinned

1 onion, sliced

juice of 1 orange

15ml/1 tbsp wholegrain mustard

30ml/2 tbsp demerara (raw) sugar

salt and ground black pepper

For the stuffing

50g/2oz spinach

50g/2oz/¼ cup dried apricots, chopped

50g/2oz Cheddar cheese, grated

1 cooking apple, peeled and grated

grated rind of ½ orange

1 Blanch the spinach in boiling water, chop, and put in a bowl with the other stuffing ingredients. Mix well together. Preheat the oven to 180°C/350°F/Gas 4.

2 Place the loin of pork, fat side down, on a board and place the stuffing down the centre. Roll the meat up and tie with cotton string. Season and put it into a roasting pan with the onion and 60ml/4 tbsp water. Cook uncovered for about 35 minutes per 450g/1lb.

3 About 40 minutes before the end of the estimated cooking time, pour off the cooking liquid into a small pan and discard the onion. Add the orange juice to the cooking liquid.

4 Spread the joint with mustard and sprinkle with the sugar. Return it to the oven and increase to 200°C/400°F/Gas 6 for 15 minutes or until crisp.

5 Meanwhile, boil up the juices and reduce to make a thin sauce. Serve with the sliced meat.

Per portion Energy 330kcal/1385kJ; Protein 49.4g; Carbohydrate 6.9g, of which sugars 6.3g; Fat 11.6g, of which saturates 4.9g; Cholesterol 145mg; Calcium 105mg; Fibre 1.2g; Sodium 227mg.

Roast pork belly with caramelized vegetables

Topped with crackling, this melting pork is served with root vegetables. The layer of fat keeps the meat moist. To ensure crisp crackling, make sure the skin is dry before roasting.

Serves 4–6

1 small swede (rutabaga), weighing about 500g/1lb 2oz

1 onion

1 parsnip

2 carrots

15ml/1 tbsp olive oil

1.5kg/3lb 6oz belly of pork, well scored

15ml/1 tbsp fresh thyme leaves or 5ml/1 tsp dried thyme

sea salt flakes and ground black pepper

Cook's tip Ask your butcher to score (slash) the pork rind really well, or use a strong sharp blade and (with care) do it yourself.

1 Preheat the oven to 220°C/425°F/ Gas 7. Cut the vegetables into small cubes (about 2cm/³⁄₄in) and stir them with the oil in a roasting pan, tossing them until evenly coated. Pour in 300ml/¹⁄₂ pint/1 ¹⁄₄ cups water.

2 Sprinkle the pork rind with thyme, salt and pepper, rubbing them well into the scored slashes in the pork belly. Place the pork on top of the vegetables, pressing it down so that it sits level, with the skin side uppermost.

3 Put the pork and vegetables into the hot oven and cook for about 30 minutes, by which time the liquid will have almost evaporated to leave a nice golden crust in the bottom of the pan. Remove the pan from the oven.

4 Add 600ml/1 pint/2½ cups cold water to the vegetables in the pan. Reduce the oven temperature to 180°C/350°F/Gas 4.

5 Cook for 1 ¹⁄₂ hours, or until the pork is tender and the juices run clear when the centre of the meat is pierced with a sharp knife. Check the oven during the final 30 minutes to make sure the liquid does not dry up, adding a little water if necessary.

6 If the crackling is not yet crisp enough, increase the oven temperature to 220°C/425°F/Gas 7 and continue cooking for another 10–20 minutes, adding extra water if necessary – just enough to prevent the vegetables from burning on the bottom of the pan.

7 With a sharp knife, slice off the crackling. Serve it with thick slices of the pork, some vegetables and the golden juices spooned over.

Per portion Energy 1014kcal/4194kJ; Protein 39.5g; Carbohydrate 9.4g, of which sugars 7.3g; Fat 91.2g, of which saturates 33.1g; Cholesterol 180mg; Calcium 81mg; Fibre 3.3g; Sodium 202mg.

Cider-glazed ham

Succulent, moist and with plenty of flavour, this old-fashioned English country recipe keeps the meat tender with a lovely sticky glaze, which is complemented by the fruit and port sauce. It is perfect to share with friends and family at Christmas or any time of the year.

Serves 8–10

2kg/4½lb middle gammon (cured ham) joint

1 large or 2 small onions

about 30 whole cloves

3 bay leaves

10 black peppercorns

1.3 litres/2½ pints/5⅔ cups medium-dry (hard) cider

45ml/3 tbsp soft light brown sugar

bunch of flat leaf parsley, to garnish

For the cranberry sauce

350g/12oz/3 cups cranberries

175g/6oz/¾ cup soft light brown sugar

grated rind and juice of 2 clementines

30ml/2 tbsp port

1 Weigh the gammon and calculate the cooking time at 20 minutes per 450g/1lb, then place it in a large flameproof casserole or pan. Stud the onion or onions with 5–10 of the cloves and add to the casserole or pan with the bay leaves and peppercorns. Add 1.2 litres/2 pints/5 cups of the cider and enough water just to cover the gammon.

2 Heat until simmering and then carefully skim off the scum that rises to the surface using a large spoon or ladle. Start timing the cooking from the moment the stock begins to simmer.

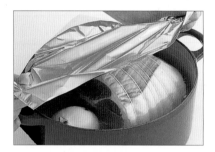

3 Cover the gammon with a lid or foil and simmer gently for the calculated time. Towards the end of the cooking time, preheat the oven to 220°C/425°F/Gas 7.

4 Heat the sugar and remaining cider in a pan; stir until the sugar has dissolved. Simmer for 5 minutes to make a dark, sticky glaze. Remove the pan from the heat and leave to cool for 5 minutes.

Cook's tips
• Leave the gammon until it is just cool enough to handle before removing the rind. Snip off the string using a sharp knife or scissors, then carefully slice off the rind, leaving a thin, even layer of fat. Use a narrow-bladed, sharp knife for the best results.
• A large stockpot is ideal for cooking a big piece of meat like this gammon, but a deep roasting pan will do in an emergency, with foil as a cover and turning the meat often for even cooking.

5 Lift the gammon out of the pan. Carefully and evenly, cut the rind from the meat, then score the fat into a diamond pattern. Place the gammon in a large roasting pan or ovenproof dish.

6 Press a clove into the centre of each diamond, then carefully spoon over the glaze. Bake for 20–25 minutes, or until the fat is brown, glistening and crisp.

7 To make the sauce, simmer all the ingredients in a pan for 20 minutes, stirring. Transfer to a jug (pitcher). Serve the gammon hot or cold, garnished with parsley and the cranberry sauce.

Per portion Energy 447kcal/1873kJ; Protein 44.1g; Carbohydrate 25.6g, of which sugars 25.6g; Fat 18.8g, of which saturates 6.3g; Cholesterol 58mg; Calcium 35mg; Fibre 1.3g; Sodium 2203mg.

Pan-fried liver with bacon, sage and onions

Calf's liver would also be ideal for this recipe, but make sure not to overcook the liver or it will become tough. Serve with green leaves and a potato and root vegetable mash. You could also try adding mashed swede, parsnip or roast pumpkin to basic mashed potatoes.

Serves 4

450g/1lb lamb's liver

30ml/2 tbsp plain (all-purpose) flour

15ml/1 tbsp oil, plus extra if necessary

8 rindless streaky (fatty) bacon rashers (slices)

2 onions, thinly sliced

4 fresh sage leaves, finely chopped

150ml/½ pint/⅔ cup chicken or vegetable stock

salt and ground black pepper

Variations
• Other liver such as venison or ox could also be used in this recipe.
• A delicious addition would be a splash of Madeira or Marsala wine to add a sweet and sticky sauce – replace the stock with the wine and bubble down.

1 Pat the liver with kitchen paper, then trim it and cut on the diagonal to make thick strips. Season the flour and toss the liver in it until it is well coated, shaking off any excess flour.

2 Heat the oil in a large frying pan and add the bacon. Cook over medium heat until the fat runs out of the bacon and it is browned and crisp. Lift out and keep warm.

3 Add the onions and sage to the frying pan. Cook over medium heat for about 10–15 minutes, stirring occasionally, until the onions are soft and golden brown.

4 Carefully lift the onions out of the pan with a draining spoon and keep them warm.

5 Increase the heat and, adding extra oil if necessary, add the liver in a single layer. Cook for 4 minutes, turning once, until browned both sides.

6 Return the onions to the pan and pour in the stock. Bring to the boil and bubble gently for a minute or two, seasoning to taste. Serve topped with the bacon.

Per portion Energy 310kcal/1293kJ; Protein 28.7g; Carbohydrate 13.7g, of which sugars 5.7g; Fat 15.9g, of which saturates 4.4g; Cholesterol 500mg; Calcium 44mg; Fibre 1.6g; Sodium 400mg.

Pot-roast ham with mustard and cabbage

An updated version of traditional boiled bacon and cabbage, this recipe also takes its inspiration from the Italian country dish of pork cooked in milk. This technique helps to counteract the saltiness of the ham, and also keeps the meat deliciously moist.

Serves 4–6

1.3kg/3lb piece of gammon (smoked or cured ham) or boiling bacon

30ml/2 tbsp oil

2 large onions, sliced

1 bay leaf

750ml/1¼ pints/3 cups milk, plus extra if necessary

15ml/1 tbsp cornflour (cornstarch), dissolved in 15ml/1 tbsp milk

45ml/3 tbsp wholegrain mustard

15–30ml/2–3 tbsp single (light) cream (optional)

1 head of cabbage, such as Savoy, trimmed, ribs removed and leaves finely sliced

ground black pepper

1 Soak the bacon joint in cold water overnight. Heat 15ml/1 tbsp oil in a pan, add the onions and cook gently.

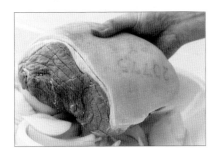

2 Place the joint on the bed of cooked onions. Add the bay leaf and milk, and season with pepper. Bring to the boil, cover and cook for about 1½ hours. Remove the meat from the pan and keep warm. Strain the cooking liquid. Reserve 300ml/½ pint/1¼ cups for the sauce and put the rest aside for soup.

3 Add the cornflour mixture to the reserved liquid and bring to the boil, stirring constantly. As it begins to thicken, stir in the wholegrain mustard and cream, if using.

4 Rinse the cabbage in cold running water and drain well.

5 Heat the remaining oil in a wok or large frying pan and stir-fry the cabbage for 2–3 minutes until cooked but still crunchy.

6 Slice the ham and serve on warmed serving plates with the mustard sauce and crisply cooked cabbage.

Per portion Energy 541kcal/2253kJ; Protein 58.4g; Carbohydrate 7.4g, of which sugars 5g; Fat 30.8g, of which saturates 9.4g; Cholesterol 77mg; Calcium 76mg; Fibre 2.1g; Sodium 2.87g.

Sausage and potato casserole

Be sure to use good meaty sausages for this traditional Irish recipe, slow cooking all the ingredients together to give the best results. Serve with some steamed buttered spinach.

Serves 4

15ml/1 tbsp vegetable oil

4 bacon rashers (strips), cut into 2.5cm/1in pieces

2 large onions, chopped

2 garlic cloves, crushed

8 large pork sausages

4 large baking potatoes, thinly sliced

1.5ml/¼ tsp fresh sage

300ml/½ pint/1¼ cups vegetable stock

salt and ground black pepper

soda bread, to serve

1 Preheat the oven to 180°C/350°F/ Gas 4. Grease a large ovenproof dish and set aside. Heat the oil in a frying pan. Add the bacon and fry for 2 minutes. Add the onions and fry for 5 minutes until golden. Add the garlic and fry for 1 minute, then remove the mixture from the pan and set aside. Then fry the sausages in the pan for 5 minutes until golden brown.

2 Arrange the potatoes in the base of the prepared dish. Spoon the bacon and onion mixture on top. Season with the salt and pepper and sprinkle with the fresh sage.

3 Pour on the stock and top with the sausages. Cover and bake for 1 hour. Serve hot with fresh soda bread.

Per portion Energy 553kcal/2305kJ; Protein 17.4g; Carbohydrate 48.7g, of which sugars 10g; Fat 33.4g, of which saturates 11.8g; Cholesterol 51mg; Calcium 74mg; Fibre 4g; Sodium 1019mg.

Toad-in-the-hole

Resembling toads peeping out of holes, this country favourite can be made with any variety of sausage. Try venison or wild boar, and replace the chives with shredded fresh sage leaves.

Serves 4–6

175g/6oz/1½ cups plain
(all-purpose) flour

30ml/2 tbsp chopped fresh chives
(optional)

2 eggs

300ml/½ pint/1¼ cups milk

50g/2oz/¼ cup white vegetable
fat or lard

450g/1lb good-quality pork sausages

salt and ground black pepper

Cook's tip To ensure really light and crisp batter, ensure that the pan is very hot before adding the batter.

1 Preheat the oven to 220°C/425°F/ Gas 7. Sift the flour into a bowl with a pinch of salt and pepper. Make a well in the centre of the flour. Whisk the chives, if using, with the eggs and milk, then pour this into the well in the flour. Gradually whisk the flour into the liquid to make a smooth batter. Cover and leave to stand for at least 30 minutes.

2 Put the fat into a small roasting pan and place in the oven for 3–5 minutes. Add the pork sausages and cook for 15 minutes. Turn the sausages twice during cooking.

3 Pour the batter over the sausages and return to the oven. Cook for about 20 minutes, or until the batter is risen and golden. Serve immediately.

Per portion Energy 497kcal/2070kJ; Protein 14.5g; Carbohydrate 32.1g, of which sugars 3.8g; Fat 35.4g, of which saturates 13.6g; Cholesterol 109mg; Calcium 141mg; Fibre 1.3g; Sodium 616mg.

Lamb stew with shallots and new potatoes

Italian gremolata made with lemon rind, garlic and parsley is a piquant garnish
for the lamb. Traditionally served with osso buco, it is also good served with fish.

Serves 6

1kg/2¼lb boneless shoulder of lamb,
trimmed of fat and cut into 5cm/
2in cubes

1 garlic clove, finely chopped

finely grated rind of ½ lemon and
juice of 1 lemon

90ml/6 tbsp olive oil

45ml/3 tbsp plain (all-purpose) flour

1 large onion, sliced

5 anchovy fillets in olive oil, drained

2.5ml/½ tsp caster (superfine) sugar

300ml/½ pint/1¼ cups white wine

475ml/16fl oz/2 cups lamb stock or
half stock and half water

1 fresh bay leaf

fresh thyme sprig

fresh parsley sprig

500g/1¼lb small new potatoes

250g/9oz shallots, peeled but
left whole

45ml/3 tbsp double (heavy)
cream (optional)

salt and ground black pepper

For the gremolata

1 garlic clove, finely chopped

finely shredded rind of ½ lemon

45ml/3 tbsp chopped fresh flat
leaf parsley

1 Mix the lamb with the garlic and the
rind and juice of ½ lemon. Season with
pepper and mix in 15ml/1 tbsp olive oil,
then leave to marinate for 12–24 hours.

2 Drain the lamb, reserving the
marinade, and pat the lamb dry with
kitchen paper. Preheat the oven to
180°C/350°F/Gas 4.

3 Heat 30ml/2 tbsp olive oil in a large,
heavy frying pan. Season the flour
with salt and pepper and toss the lamb
in it to coat, shaking off any excess.
Seal the lamb on all sides in the hot
oil. Do this in batches, transferring
each batch of lamb to an ovenproof
pan or flameproof casserole as you
brown it. You may need to add an
extra 15ml/1 tbsp olive oil to the pan.

4 Reduce the heat, add another
15ml/1 tbsp oil to the pan and cook
the onion gently over a very low heat,
stirring frequently, for 10 minutes, until
softened and golden but not browned.

5 Add the anchovies and caster sugar,
and cook, mashing the anchovies into
the soft onion with a wooden spoon
until well combined.

6 Add the reserved marinade, increase
the heat a little and cook for about
1–2 minutes, then pour in the wine
and stock or stock and water and bring
to the boil. Simmer gently for about
5 minutes, then pour over the lamb.

7 Tie the bay leaf, thyme and parsley
together and add to the lamb. Season
with salt and pepper, then cover tightly
and cook in the oven for 1 hour. Stir
the potatoes into the stew and cook
for a further 20 minutes.

8 Meanwhile, to make the gremolata,
chop all the ingredients together finely.
Place in a dish, cover and set aside.

9 Heat the remaining oil in a frying
pan and brown the shallots on all
sides, then stir them into the lamb.

10 Cover and cook for a further
30–40 minutes, until the lamb is
tender. Transfer the lamb and
vegetables to a dish and keep
warm. Discard the herbs.

11 Boil the cooking juices to reduce and
concentrate them, then add the cream,
if using, and simmer for 2–3 minutes.

12 Adjust the seasoning, adding a little
lemon juice to taste. Pour this sauce
over the lamb, sprinkle the gremolata
on top and serve immediately.

Per portion Energy 553kcal/2311kJ; Protein 37g; Carbohydrate 26.2g, of which sugars 5.3g; Fat 30.6g, of which saturates 10.4g; Cholesterol 128mg; Calcium 79mg; Fibre 2.7g; Sodium 261mg.

Rib of beef with Yorkshire puddings

A quintessential Sunday-lunch classic, this is the well-loved 'roast beef of old England', traditionally served with crisp Yorkshire puddings, golden roast potatoes and a selection of seasonal green and root vegetables, all covered in mouth-watering gravy and accompanied by a tangy horseradish cream. In Yorkshire the puddings are often served before the meat, with the gravy, as a first course. Either way, this dish will have your guests asking for more.

Serves 6–8

rib of beef joint, weighing about 3kg/6½lb

oil, for brushing

salt and ground black pepper

For the Yorkshire puddings

115g/4oz/1 cup plain (all-purpose) flour

1.5ml/¼ tsp salt

1 egg

200ml/7fl oz/scant 1 cup milk

oil or beef dripping, for greasing

For the horseradish cream

60–75ml/4–5 tbsp finely grated fresh horseradish

300ml/½ pint/1¼ cups sour cream

30ml/2 tbsp cider vinegar or white wine vinegar

10ml/2 tsp caster (superfine) sugar

For the gravy

600ml/1 pint/2½ cups good beef stock

Cook's tip To avoid the pungent smell (and tears) produced by grating horseradish, use a jar of preserved grated horseradish.

1 Preheat the oven to 220°C/425°F/ Gas 7. Weigh the joint and calculate the cooking time required as follows: 10–15 minutes per 500g/1¼lb for rare beef, 15–20 minutes for medium and 20–25 minutes for well done.

2 Put the joint into a large roasting pan. Brush it all over with oil and season with salt and pepper. Put into the hot oven and cook for 30 minutes, until the beef is browned. Lower the oven temperature to 160°C/325°F/Gas 3 and cook for the calculated time, spooning the juices over the meat occasionally during cooking.

3 For the Yorkshire pudding, sift the flour and salt into a bowl and break the egg into it. Make the milk up to 300ml/½ pint/1¼ cups with water and gradually whisk into the flour to make a smooth batter. Leave to stand while the beef cooks. Generously grease eight Yorkshire pudding tins (muffin pans) measuring about 10cm/4in.

4 For the horseradish cream, put all the ingredients into a bowl and mix well. Cover and chill until required.

5 At the end of its cooking time, remove the beef from the oven, cover with foil and leave to stand for 30–40 minutes while you cook the Yorkshire puddings and make the gravy.

6 Increase the oven temperature to 220°C/425°F/Gas 7 and put the prepared tins on the top shelf for 5 minutes until very hot. Pour in the batter and cook for about 15 minutes until well risen, crisp and golden brown.

7 To make the gravy, transfer the beef to a warmed serving plate. Pour off the fat from the roasting pan, leaving the meat juices. Add the stock to the pan, bring to the boil and bubble until reduced by about half. Season to taste.

8 Carve the beef and serve with the gravy, Yorkshire puddings, roast potatoes and horseradish cream.

Per portion Energy 1037kcal/4338kJ; Protein 129g; Carbohydrate 15.1g, of which sugars 4.1g; Fat 51.5g, of which saturates 24.3g; Cholesterol 352mg; Calcium 123mg; Fibre 0.5g; Sodium 249mg.

Pot roast beef with stout

Use a boned and rolled joint such as brisket, silverside or topside for this slow-cooked dish, where the vegetables are cooked with the beef and the meat becomes meltingly tender.

Serves 6

30ml/2 tbsp vegetable oil

900g/2lb rolled brisket of beef

2 medium onions, roughly chopped

2 celery sticks, thickly sliced

450g/1lb carrots, cut into large chunks

675g/1½lb potatoes, peeled and cut into large chunks

30ml/2 tbsp plain (all-purpose) flour

450ml/¾ pint/ 2 cups beef stock

300ml/½ pint/1¼ cups stout

1 bay leaf

45ml/3 tbsp chopped fresh thyme

5ml/1 tsp soft light brown sugar

30ml/2 tbsp wholegrain mustard

15ml/1 tbsp tomato purée (paste)

salt and ground black pepper

3 Add the celery, carrots and potatoes to the casserole and cook over a medium heat for 2–3 minutes, or until they are just beginning to colour.

4 Add the flour and cook for a further 1 minute, stirring constantly. Gradually pour in the beef stock and the stout. Heat until the mixture comes to the boil, stirring frequently.

5 Stir in the bay leaf, thyme, sugar, mustard, tomato purée and seasoning. Place the meat on top, cover tightly and transfer the casserole to the hot oven.

6 Cook for about 2½ hours, or until tender. Adjust the seasoning, to taste. To serve, carve the beef into thick slices and serve with the vegetables and plenty of gravy.

1 Preheat the oven to 180°C/350°F/ Gas 4. Heat the oil in a large flameproof casserole and brown the beef until golden brown all over.

2 Lift the beef from the pan and drain on kitchen paper. Add the onions to the pan and cook for about 4 minutes, until just beginning to soften and brown.

Per portion Energy 415kcal/1743kJ; Protein 36g; Carbohydrate 35.6g, of which sugars 13.1g; Fat 14g, of which saturates 4.4g; Cholesterol 81mg; Calcium 66mg; Fibre 4.2g; Sodium 284mg.

Braised beef and country vegetables

A dish which, in the past, would have been gently left to cook all day, this casserole is just as impressive slow cooked for a few hours. It is delicious with suet dumplings or crusty bread.

Serves 4–6

1kg/2¼lb lean stewing steak, cut into 5cm/2in cubes

45ml/3 tbsp plain (all-purpose) flour

45ml/3 tbsp oil

1 large onion, thinly sliced

1 large carrot, thickly sliced

2 celery sticks, finely chopped

300ml/½ pint/¼ cup beef stock

30ml/2 tbsp tomato purée (paste)

5ml/1 tsp dried mixed herbs

15ml/1 tbsp dark muscovado (molasses) sugar

225g/8oz baby potatoes, halved

2 leeks, thinly sliced

salt and ground black pepper

Variation Replace the potatoes with dumplings. Sift 175g/6oz/1½ cups self-raising (self-rising) flour and stir in 75g/3oz/½ cup shredded suet (US chilled, grated shortening), 30ml/2 tbsp chopped parsley and seasoning. Stir in water to make a soft dough and divide the mixture into 12 balls. In step 6, stir in the leeks and put the dumplings on top. Cover and cook for 15–20 minutes more.

1 Preheat the oven to 150°C/300°F/ Gas 2. Season the flour and use to coat the beef cubes.

2 Heat the oil in a large, flameproof casserole. Add a small batch of meat, cook quickly until browned on all sides and, with a slotted spoon, lift out. Repeat with the remaining beef.

3 Add the onion, carrot and celery to the casserole. Cook over medium heat for about 10 minutes, stirring frequently, until they begin to soften and brown slightly on the edges.

4 Return the meat to the casserole and add the stock, tomato purée, herbs and sugar, at the same time scraping up any sediment that has stuck to the casserole. Heat until the liquid nearly comes to the boil.

5 Cover with a tight fitting lid and put into the hot oven. Cook for 2–2½ hours, or until the beef is tender.

6 Gently stir in the potatoes and leeks, cover and continue cooking for a further 30 minutes or until the potatoes are soft.

Per portion Energy 450kcal/1880kJ; Protein 41.3g; Carbohydrate 23.6g, of which sugars 10.3g; Fat 21.7g, of which saturates 7.3g; Cholesterol 97mg; Calcium 63mg; Fibre 3.5g; Sodium 137mg.

Boeuf Bourguignon

Beef cooked 'Burgundy style' in red wine with chopped bacon, baby onions and mushrooms and simmered for hours at a low temperature produces a rich, dark gravy and melt-in-the-mouth meat. Serve with creamy mashed potato and croûtons of bread fried in duck fat.

Serves 6

175g/6oz rindless streaky (fatty) bacon rashers (strips), chopped

900g/2lb lean braising steak, such as top rump of beef or braising steak

30ml/2 tbsp plain (all-purpose) flour

45ml/3 tbsp sunflower oil

25g/1oz/2 tbsp butter

12 shallots

2 garlic cloves, crushed

175g/6oz/2½ cups mushrooms, sliced

450ml/¾ pint/scant 2 cups robust red wine

150ml/¼ pint/⅔ cup beef stock or consommé

1 bay leaf

2 sprigs each of fresh thyme, parsley and marjoram

salt and ground black pepper

Variation Instead of the rindless streaky (fatty) bacon rashers (strips), use lardons, which are available from supermarkets.

1 Preheat the oven to 160°C/325°F/ Gas 3. Heat a large flameproof casserole, then add the bacon and cook, stirring occasionally, until the pieces are crisp and golden brown.

2 Meanwhile, cut the meat into 2.5cm/ 1in cubes. Season the flour and use to coat the meat. Use a draining spoon to remove the bacon from the casserole and set aside. Add and heat the oil, then brown the beef in batches and set aside with the bacon.

3 Add the butter to the fat remaining in the casserole. Cook the shallots and crushed garlic until just starting to colour, then add the sliced mushrooms and cook for a further 5 minutes. Replace the bacon and meat, and stir in the wine and stock or consommé. Tie the bay leaf, thyme, parsley and marjoram together into a bouquet garni and add to the casserole.

4 Cover and cook in the oven for 1½ hours, or until the meat is tender, stirring once or twice. Season to taste and serve the casserole with creamy mashed root vegetables, such as celeriac and potatoes.

Cook's tip Boeuf Bourguignon freezes very well. Transfer the mixture to a dish so that it cools quickly, then pour it into a rigid plastic container. Push all the cubes of meat down into the sauce or they will dry out. Freeze for up to 2 months. Thaw overnight in the refrigerator, then transfer to a flameproof casserole and add 150ml/ ¼ pint/⅔ cup water. Stir well, bring to the boil, stirring occasionally, and simmer steadily for at least 10 minutes, or until the meat is piping hot.

Per portion Energy 749kcal/3117kJ; Protein 63.3g; Carbohydrate 15.2g, of which sugars 8.8g; Fat 40.3g, of which saturates 14g; Cholesterol 167mg; Calcium 69mg; Fibre 2.8g; Sodium 868mg.

Braised oxtail

While oxtail requires long, slow cooking to tenderize the meat, the resulting complex, dark flavours are well worth the effort. This dish is traditionally served with plain boiled potatoes to soak up the rich gravy, though mashed potatoes would be good too.

Serves 6

2 oxtails, trimmed, cut into pieces, total weight about 1.5kg/3lb 6oz

30ml/2 tbsp flour seasoned with salt and pepper

45ml/3 tbsp oil

2 large onions, sliced

2 celery sticks, sliced

4 medium carrots, sliced

1 litre/1¾ pints/4 cups beef stock

15ml/1 tbsp tomato purée (paste)

finely grated rind of 1 small orange

2 bay leaves

few sprigs of fresh thyme

salt and ground black pepper

chopped fresh parsley, to garnish

1 Preheat the oven to 150°C/300°F/Gas 2. Coat the pieces of oxtail in the seasoned flour, shaking off and reserving any excess.

2 Heat 30ml/2 tbsp oil in a large flameproof casserole and add the oxtail in batches, cooking quickly until browned all over. Lift out and set aside. Add the remaining oil to the pan, and stir in the onions, celery and carrots.

3 Cook the vegetables quickly, stirring occasionally, until beginning to brown. Tip in any reserved flour, then add the stock, tomato purée and orange rind.

Cook's tip This dish benefits from being made in advance. When cooled completely, any fat can be removed before reheating.

4 Heat until bubbles begin to rise to the surface, then add the herbs, cover and put into the hot oven. Cook for 3½–4 hours until the oxtail is very tender.

5 Remove from the oven and leave to stand, covered, for 10 minutes before skimming off the surface fat. Adjust the seasoning and garnish with parsley.

Per portion Energy 341kcal/1426kJ; Protein 30.9g; Carbohydrate 13.6g, of which sugars 7.7g; Fat 18.6g, of which saturates 0.7g; Cholesterol 0mg; Calcium 54mg; Fibre 2.3g; Sodium 203mg.

Beef in red wine with a potato crust

This recipe makes the best of braising beef by marinating it in red wine and topping it with a cheesy grated potato crust that bakes to a golden, crunchy consistency. For a change, instead of grating the potatoes, slice them thinly and layer over the top of the beef with onion rings and crushed garlic. The dish makes a satistfying meal on its own.

Serves 4

675g/1½lb stewing beef, diced

300ml/½ pint/1¼ cups red wine

3 juniper berries, crushed

slice of orange peel

30ml/2 tbsp olive oil

2 onions, cut into chunks

2 carrots, cut into chunks

1 garlic clove, crushed

225g/8oz/3 cups button (white) mushrooms

150ml/¼ pint/⅔ cup beef stock

30ml/2 tbsp cornflour (cornstarch)

salt and ground black pepper

For the crust

450g/1lb potatoes, grated

15ml/1 tbsp olive oil

30ml/2 tbsp creamed horseradish

50g/2oz/½ cup mature (sharp) Cheddar cheese, grated

salt and ground black pepper

1 Place the diced beef in a non-metallic bowl. Add the wine, berries, and orange peel and season with pepper. Mix the ingredients, then cover and leave to marinate for at least 4 hours or overnight.

2 Preheat the oven to 160°C/325°F/Gas 3. Drain the beef, reserving the marinade.

3 Heat the oil in a large flameproof casserole and fry the meat in batches for 5 minutes to seal. Add the onions, carrots and garlic and cook for 5 minutes. Stir in the mushrooms, red wine marinade and beef stock. Simmer.

4 Mix the cornflour with water to make a smooth paste. Stir into the pan. Season, cover and cook for 1½ hours.

5 Make the crust 30 minutes before the end of the cooking time for the beef. Start by blanching the grated potatoes in boiling water for 5 minutes. Drain well and then squeeze out all the extra liquid.

6 Stir in the remaining ingredients and then sprinkle evenly over the surface of the beef. Increase the oven temperature to 200°C/400°F/Gas 6 and cook the dish for a further 30 minutes so that the top is crispy and slightly browned.

Cook's tip Use a large grater on the food processor for the potatoes, or alternatively, grate them by hand with a traditional grater. They will hold their shape better while being blanched than if you use a finer blade.

Per portion Energy 474kcal/1973kJ; Protein 43g; Carbohydrate 6.1g, of which sugars 5.6g; Fat 28.8g, of which saturates 8.7g; Cholesterol 106mg; Calcium 53mg; Fibre 2.6g; Sodium 564mg.

Steak, mushroom and ale pie

This dish is a firm favourite on menus at restaurants specializing in traditional country fare. Preparing the filling the day before and allowing the meat and vegetables to rest overnight ensures a particularly tasty filling. The pie can be ready relatively quickly simply by topping with the pastry and baking. Serve with seasonal vegetables or a side salad.

Serves 4

25g/1oz/2 tbsp butter

1 large onion, finely chopped

115g/4oz/1½ cups chestnut or button (white) mushrooms, halved

900g/2lb lean beef in one piece, such as rump or braising steak

30ml/2 tbsp plain (all-purpose) flour

45ml/3 tbsp sunflower oil

300ml/½ pint/1¼ cups stout or brown ale

300ml/½ pint/1¼ cups beef stock or consommé

500g/1¼lb puff pastry, thawed if frozen

beaten egg, to glaze

salt and ground black pepper

1 Melt the butter in a large, flameproof casserole, add the onion and cook gently, stirring occasionally, for about 5 minutes, or until it is softened. Add the halved mushrooms and continue cooking for a further 5 minutes, stirring.

2 Meanwhile, trim the meat and cut it into 2.5cm/1in cubes. Season the flour and toss the meat in it.

3 Remove the onion mixture from the casserole and set aside. Add the oil, then brown the steak in batches.

4 Replace the vegetables, then stir in the stout or ale and stock or consommé. Bring to the boil, reduce the heat and simmer for 1 hour, stirring occasionally. Season to taste and transfer to a 1.5 litre/2½ pint/6½ cup pie dish. Cover and leave to cool. If possible, chill the meat filling overnight, as this allows the flavour to develop. Preheat the oven to 230°C/450°F/Gas 8.

5 Roll out the pastry in the shape of the dish and about 4cm/1½in larger all around. Cut a 2.5cm/1in strip from the edge of the pastry. Brush the rim of the dish with water and press the pastry strip on it. Brush the pastry rim with beaten egg and cover the pie with the pastry lid. Press the lid firmly in place, then trim of the excess.

6 Use the blunt edge of a knife to tap the outside edge of the pastry, pressing it down with your finger as you seal in the filling. (This technique is known as knocking up.)

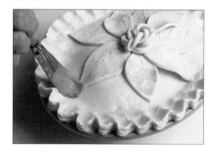

7 Pinch the pastry between your fingers to flute the edge. Roll out any remaining pastry trimmings and cut out shapes to garnish the pie, brushing the shapes with a little beaten egg before pressing them lightly in place.

8 Make a hole in the middle of the pie to allow steam to escape, brush the top carefully with beaten egg and chill for 10 minutes to rest the pastry.

9 Bake the pie for 15 minutes, then reduce the oven temperature to 200°C/400°F/Gas 6 and bake for a further 15–20 minutes, or until the pastry is risen and golden. Let the pie rest for a minute or two before serving.

Per portion Energy 1061kcal/4423kJ; Protein 58.8g; Carbohydrate 59.3g, of which sugars 7.6g; Fat 65.3g, of which saturates 24g; Cholesterol 164mg; Calcium 129mg; Fibre 3.2g; Sodium 622mg.

Steak and kidney pudding

One of the best-known English country dishes, this tasty pudding is a 19th-century recipe that originally contained oysters, but mushrooms are more often used today. Although it has a relatively long cooking time, the finished result is well worth the wait.

Serves 6

500g/1¼lb lean stewing steak, cut into cubes

225g/8oz beef kidney or lamb's kidneys, skin and core removed and cut into small cubes

1 medium onion, finely chopped

30ml/2 tbsp finely chopped fresh herbs, such as parsley and thyme

30ml/2 tbsp plain (all-purpose) flour

275g/10oz/2½ cups self-raising (self-rising) flour

150g/5oz/1 cup shredded suet (US chilled, grated shortening)

finely grated rind of 1 small lemon

about 120ml/4fl oz/½ cup beef stock or water

salt and ground black pepper

1 Put the stewing steak into a large bowl and add the kidneys, onion and chopped herbs. Sprinkle the plain flour and seasoning over the top and mix well.

2 To make the pastry, sift the self-raising flour into another large bowl. Stir in the suet and lemon rind. Add sufficient cold water to bind the ingredients and gather into a soft dough.

3 On a lightly floured surface, knead the dough gently, and then roll out to make a circle measuring about 35cm/14in across. Cut out one-quarter of the circle, roll up and put aside.

4 Lightly butter a 1.75 litre/3 pint heatproof bowl. Line the bowl with the rolled out dough, pressing the cut edges together and allowing the pastry to overlap the top of the bowl slightly.

5 Spoon the steak mixture into the lined bowl, packing it in carefully, so as not to split the pastry.

6 Pour in sufficient stock to reach no more than three-quarters of the way up the filling. (Any stock remaining can be heated and poured into the cooked pudding to thin the gravy if desired.)

7 Roll out the reserved pastry into a circle to form a lid and lay it over the filling, pinching the edges together to seal them well.

8 Cover with baking parchment, pleated in the centre to allow the pudding to rise, then cover again with a large sheet of foil (again pleated at the centre). Tuck the edges under and press them tightly to the sides of the basin until securely sealed (alternatively, tie with string). Steam for about 5 hours.

9 Carefully remove the foil and paper, slide a knife around the sides of the pudding and turn out on to a warmed serving plate.

Per portion Energy 436kcal/1835kJ; Protein 31.1g; Carbohydrate 49.5g, of which sugars 4.8g; Fat 13.9g, of which saturates 3.6g; Cholesterol 166mg; Calcium 201mg; Fibre 1.9g; Sodium 380mg.

Veal casserole with broad beans

This delicate stew, flavoured with sherry and plenty of garlic, is a spring casserole made with new vegetables – menestra de ternera. For a delicious flavour, be sure to add plenty of parsley just before serving. Lamb would be equally good cooked in this way.

Serves 6

45ml/3 tbsp olive oil

1.3–1.6kg/3–3½lb veal, cut into 5cm/2in cubes

1 large onion, chopped

6 large garlic cloves, unpeeled

1 bay leaf

5ml/1 tsp paprika

250ml/8fl oz/1 cup fino sherry

100g/4oz/scant 1 cup shelled, skinned broad (fava) beans

60ml/4 tbsp fresh flat leaf parsley

salt and ground black pepper

1 Heat 30ml/2 tbsp oil in a large flameproof casserole. Add half the meat and brown well on all sides. Transfer to a plate. Brown the rest of the meat and remove from the pan.

2 Add the remaining oil to the pan and cook the onion until soft. Return the meat to the casserole and stir well to mix with the onion.

3 Add the garlic cloves, bay leaf, paprika and sherry. Season. Bring to simmering point, then cover and cook very gently for 30–40 minutes.

4 Add the broad beans to the casserole about 10 minutes before the end of the cooking time. Chop the flat leaf parsley. Check the seasoning and stir in the parsley just before serving.

Per portion Energy 352kcal/1473kJ; Protein 47.4g; Carbohydrate 3.6g, of which sugars 1.3g; Fat 11.6g, of which saturates 2.8g; Cholesterol 182mg; Calcium 34mg; Fibre 1.2g; Sodium 244mg.

Veal and ham pie

Historically, the English love pies made with mutton and pork. This splendid version contains diced veal, gammon and hard-boiled eggs. The flavours of the two meats marry perfectly in the delicate filling. Serve with green cabbage leaves and buttery mashed potato.

Serves 4

450g/1lb boneless shoulder
of veal, diced

225g/8oz lean gammon (smoked
or cured ham), diced

15ml/1 tbsp plain (all-purpose) flour

large pinch each of dry mustard
and ground black pepper

25g/1oz/2 tbsp butter

15ml/1 tbsp sunflower oil

1 onion, chopped

600ml/1 pint/2½ cups chicken
or veal stock

2 eggs, hard-boiled and sliced

30ml/2 tbsp chopped fresh parsley

For the pastry

175g/6oz/1½ cups plain
(all-purpose) flour

75g/3oz/6 tbsp butter

iced water, to mix

beaten egg, to glaze

1 Preheat the oven to 180°C/350°F/ Gas 4. Mix the veal and gammon in a bowl. Season the flour with the mustard and pepper, then add it to the meat and toss well. Heat the butter and oil in a casserole until sizzling, then cook the meat mixture in batches until golden on all sides. Remove the meat from the pan.

2 Cook the onion in the fat remaining in the casserole until softened, but not coloured. Gradually stir in the stock, then replace the meat mixture and stir. Cover and cook in the oven for 1½ hours, or until the veal is tender.

3 To make the pastry, sift the flour into a bowl and rub in the butter with your fingers. Mix in enough iced water to bind the mixture into clumps, then press these together with your fingertips to make a dough.

4 Spoon the cooked veal and gammon mixture into a 1.5 litre/2½ pint/6¼ cup pie dish. Arrange the slices of hard-boiled egg over the top and sprinkle with the chopped parsley.

5 Roll out the pastry on a lightly floured work surface to about 4cm/1½in larger than the top of the pie dish.

6 Cover the pie dish with the pastry lid. Press the pastry around the rim to seal in the filling and cut off any excess. Use the blunt edge of a knife to tap the outside edge of the pastry, pressing it down with your finger as you seal in the filling. Pinch the pastry between your fingers to flute the edge.

7 Roll out any remaining pastry and cut out decorative shapes to garnish the top of the pie. Brush with beaten egg and bake for 30–40 minutes, or until the pastry is well-risen and golden brown. Serve hot with steamed green cabbage and creamy mashed potato.

Per portion Energy 621kcal/2595kJ; Protein 42.4g; Carbohydrate 39.2g, of which sugars 2.6g; Fat 33.8g, of which saturates 17.2g; Cholesterol 281mg; Calcium 128mg; Fibre 2.3g; Sodium 1007mg.

Vegetable side dishes

Tasty and nutritious, vegetables are vital to good health and well-being. Served simply with a little unsalted butter or a drizzle of olive oil and a scatter of chopped herbs, they are hard to beat. Seasonal treats such as asparagus and new potatoes are best eaten as fresh as possible, so always seek out local suppliers or enrol in a vegetable box scheme that will give access to what's in season.

Spring vegetables with tarragon

This is almost a salad since the vegetables are only lightly cooked. The bright, fresh flavours are enhanced with the aniseed flavour of tarragon. Serve alongside fish, seafood or chicken.

Serves 4

5 spring onions (scallions)

50g/2oz/¼ cup butter

1 garlic clove, crushed

115g/4oz asparagus tips

115g/4oz mangetouts (snowpeas), trimmed

115g/4oz broad (fava) beans

2 Little Gem (Bibb) lettuces

5ml/1 tsp finely chopped fresh tarragon

salt and ground black pepper

1 Cut the spring onions into quarters lengthways and fry gently over a medium-low heat in half the butter with the garlic.

2 Add the asparagus tips, mangetouts and broad beans. Mix the vegetables gently, making sure they are all well coated in oil.

3 Just cover the base of the pan with water, season, and allow to simmer gently for a few minutes, until the vegetables are tender.

4 Cut the lettuce into quarters and add to the pan. Cook for 3 minutes then, off the heat, swirl in the remaining butter and the tarragon, and serve.

Per portion Energy 149kcal/619kJ; Protein 4.7g; Carbohydrate 6.1g, of which sugars 3g; Fat 12g, of which saturates 7.3g; Cholesterol 29mg; Calcium 55mg; Fibre 3.5g; Sodium 89mg.

Fresh green beans and tomato sauce

A standard country summer dish in Greece made with whichever beans are available, this pretty side dish is most often served with feta cheese, olives and flat bread.

Serves 4

800g/1¾lb green beans, trimmed

150ml/¼ pint/⅔ cup extra virgin olive oil

1 large onion, thinly sliced

2 garlic cloves, chopped

2 small potatoes, peeled and chopped into cubes

675g/1½lb tomatoes or a 400g/14oz can plum tomatoes, chopped

150ml/¼ pint/⅔ cup hot water

45–60ml/3–4 tbsp chopped fresh parsley

salt and ground black pepper

1 If the green beans are very long, cut them in half. Drop them into a bowl of cold water so that they are completely submerged. Leave them to absorb the water for a few minutes. To test if the beans are fresh, snap one in half. If it breaks crisply it is fresh; if it bends rather than breaking, the beans are not fresh.

2 Heat the olive oil in a large pan, add the onion and sauté until translucent. Add the garlic, then, when it becomes aromatic, stir in the potatoes and sauté the mixture for a few minutes.

3 Add the tomatoes and the hot water and cook for 5 minutes. Drain the beans, rinse them and drain again, then add them to the pan with a little salt and pepper to season. Cover and simmer for 30 minutes.

4 Stir in the chopped parsley, with a little more hot water if the mixture is dry. Cook for 10 minutes more, until the beans are very tender. Serve hot with slices of feta cheese, if you like.

Per portion Energy 350kcal/1,448kJ; Protein 6.6g; Carbohydrate 21.9g, of which sugars 13.4g; Fat 26.9g, of which saturates 4g; Cholesterol 0mg; Calcium 121mg; Fibre 7.7g; Sodium 25mg.

Sautéed broad beans with bacon

Particularly associated with Andalucía, where broad beans are served to bulls destined for the bullring, this classic country dish is eaten all over Spain. Use young tender broad beans or, if using larger beans, remove the skins to reveal the bright green inner bean.

Serves 4

30ml/2 tbsp olive oil

1 small onion, finely chopped

1 garlic clove, finely chopped

50g/2oz rindless smoked streaky (fatty) bacon, roughly chopped

225g/8oz broad (fava) beans, thawed if frozen

5ml/1 tsp paprika

15ml/1 tbsp sweet sherry

salt and ground black pepper

1 Heat the olive oil in a large frying pan or sauté pan. Add the chopped onion, garlic and bacon and fry over a high heat for about 5 minutes, stirring frequently, until the onion is softened and the bacon browned.

2 Add the beans and paprika to the pan and stir-fry for 1 minute. Add the sherry, lower the heat, cover and cook for 5–10 minutes until the beans are tender. Season with salt and pepper to taste and serve hot or warm.

Per portion Energy 139kcal/577kJ; Protein 6.8g; Carbohydrate 8.2g, of which sugars 1.6g; Fat 9g, of which saturates 1.9g; Cholesterol 8mg; Calcium 38mg; Fibre 3.9g; Sodium 163mg.

Creamed leeks

Versatile leeks are a great winter vegetable, adding a subtle onion flavour to many dishes, including soups, casseroles, stews and stir-fries. Serve these creamed leeks on their own, or as a tasty accompaniment to grilled meats, such as chops, chicken or gammon.

Serves 4–6

4 large or 8 medium leeks

300ml/½ pint/1¼ cups milk

8 streaky (fatty) rashers (strips) of bacon, trimmed and sliced (optional)

1 egg, lightly beaten

150ml/¼ pint/⅔ cup single (light) cream

15ml/1 tbsp mild Irish mustard

75g/3oz/¾ cup grated cheese (optional)

salt and ground black pepper

1 Slice the leeks into fairly large chunks. Put them into a pan with the milk. Season and bring to the boil. Reduce the heat and simmer for 15–20 minutes, or until tender. Drain well and turn the leeks into a buttered shallow baking dish, reserving the cooking liquor.

2 Meanwhile, if using the bacon, put it into a frying pan and cook gently to allow the fat to run, then turn up the heat a little and cook for a few minutes until it crisps up. Remove from the pan with a slotted spoon and sprinkle the bacon over the leeks.

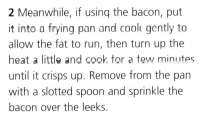

3 Rinse the pan used for the leeks. Blend the beaten egg, single cream and Irish mustard together and mix it with the reserved cooking liquor. Return to the pan and heat gently without boiling, allowing the sauce to thicken a little. Taste and adjust the seasoning with salt and ground black pepper. Pour the sauce over the leeks and bacon.

4 Sprinkle the baking dish with grated cheese, if using, and brown for a few minutes under a hot grill (broiler). (Alternatively, the leeks may be served immediately without browning them.) Serve with plain grilled (broiled) meat or poultry, if you like.

Variations
• The bacon may be grilled (broiled) and served separately, if you prefer.
• Omit the cheese topping and use the leeks and bacon to dress hot tagliatelle or spaghetti, or use in a risotto.
• The leeks could also be spread on to toast topped with cheese and grilled for a light lunch.

Per portion Energy 238kcal/993kJ; Protein 18.6g; Carbohydrate 9g, of which sugars 7.9g; Fat 14.4g, of which saturates 7.3g; Cholesterol 90mg; Calcium 172mg; Fibre 3.5g; Sodium 830mg.

Butter-braised lettuce, peas and spring onions

A well-loved French country recipe, this dish is traditionally served with grilled fish or meat. Try adding shredded fresh mint or substituting mangetouts or sugar snaps for the peas.

Serves 4

50g/2oz/¼ cup butter

4 Little Gem (Bibb) lettuces, halved lengthways

2 bunches spring onions (scallions), trimmed

400g/14oz shelled peas (about 1kg/2¼lb in pods)

salt and ground black pepper

Variations
• Braise about 250g/9oz baby carrots with the lettuce.
• Cook 115g/4oz chopped smoked bacon in the butter. Use 1 bunch spring onions (scallions) and some chopped parsley.

1 Melt half the butter in a wide, heavy pan over a low heat. Add the lettuces and spring onions.

2 Turn the vegetables in the butter, then sprinkle in salt and plenty of ground black pepper. Cover, and cook the vegetables very gently for 5 minutes, stirring once.

3 Add the peas and turn them in the buttery juices. Pour in 120ml/4fl oz/ ½ cup water, then cover and cook over a gentle heat for a further 5 minutes. Uncover and increase the heat to reduce the liquid to a few tablespoons.

4 Stir in the remaining butter. Transfer to a warmed serving dish and serve.

Per portion Energy 161kcal/670kJ; Protein 9.1g; Carbohydrate 15.9g, of which sugars 6.8g; Fat 7.4g, of which saturates 3.7g; Cholesterol 13mg; Calcium 73mg; Fibre 6.5g; Sodium 47mg.

Cauliflower cheese

A mature, strong farmhouse cheddar cheese gives an authentic taste to this simple country classic, or try making this recipe with half cauliflower and half broccoli florets.

Serves 4

1 medium cauliflower

25g/1oz/2 tbsp butter

25g/1oz/4 tbsp plain (all-purpose) flour

300ml/½ pint/1¼ cups milk

115g/4oz mature (sharp) Cheddar or Cheshire cheese, grated

salt and ground black pepper

1 Trim the cauliflower and cut it into florets. Bring a pan of lightly salted water to the boil, drop in the cauliflower and cook for 5–8 minutes or until just tender. Drain and transfer the florets into an ovenproof dish.

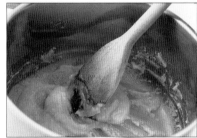

2 To make the sauce, melt the butter in a pan, stir in the flour and cook gently, stirring constantly, for about 1 minute (do not allow it to brown). Remove from the heat and gradually stir in the milk. Return the pan to the heat and cook, stirring, until the mixture thickens and comes to the boil. Simmer gently for 1–2 minutes.

3 Stir in three-quarters of the cheese and season to taste. Spoon the sauce over the cauliflower and sprinkle the remaining cheese on top. Put under a hot grill (broiler) until golden brown.

Cook's tip Boost the cheese flavour by adding a little English (hot) mustard to the cheese sauce.

Per portion Energy 318kcal/1318kJ; Protein 17.4g; Carbohydrate 4.4g, of which sugars 3.9g; Fat 25.8g, of which saturates 16.3g; Cholesterol 71mg; Calcium 371mg; Fibre 1.8g; Sodium 453mg.

Asparagus with hollandaise sauce

The asparagus season is short, and this country dish makes the most of its delicate and distinctive flavour. Asparagus can be served simply with melted butter drizzled over the top, but this delicious whisked white wine hollandaise sauce makes it really special.

Serves 4

2 bunches of asparagus

30ml/2 tbsp white wine vinegar

2 egg yolks

115g/4oz butter, melted

juice of ½ lemon

salt and ground black pepper

Cook's tips
• Asparagus should be cooked and eaten as soon as possible, preferably on the day it is picked.
• Make stock with the woody ends of the asparagus rather than throwing them away and add it to vegetable soups or sauces, or use for risotto.

1 Snap off the tough ends of the asparagus. Drop the spears into fast boiling water, cooking for 1–2 minutes until just tender. Test the thickest part of the stalk with a small sharp knife; take care not to overcook.

2 In a pan, bring the vinegar to the boil and bubble until it has reduced to just 15ml/1 tbsp. Remove from the heat and add 15ml/1 tbsp cold water.

3 Whisk the egg yolks into the vinegar and water mixture, then put the pan over a very low heat and continue whisking until the mixture is frothy and thickened.

4 Remove from the heat again and slowly whisk in the melted butter. Add the lemon juice and seasoning to taste. Serve the sauce immediately with the drained asparagus.

Per portion Energy 276kcal/1135kJ; Protein 5.3g; Carbohydrate 2.7g, of which sugars 2.6g; Fat 27.1g, of which saturates 15.9g; Cholesterol 162mg; Calcium 51mg; Fibre 2.1g; Sodium 180mg.

Jerusalem artichokes au gratin

An under-appreciated vegetable, the Jerusalem artichoke – sometimes known as the 'sun choke' – has a distinctive nutty flavour and an appealing crunch. This creamy gratin side dish is the perfect accompaniment to roast meat or fried fish.

Serves 4

250ml/8fl oz/1 cup sour cream

50ml/2fl oz/¼ cup single (light) cream

675g/1½lb Jerusalem artichokes, coarsely chopped

40g/1½oz/½ cup grated Danbo cheese

60ml/4 tbsp fresh breadcrumbs

salt

Variation If you can't find Danbo, a mellow yet flavoursome semi-hard cheese, look for Elbo, Havarti, or use a good English Cheddar.

1 Preheat the oven to 190°C/375°F/ Gas 5. Lightly grease an ovenproof dish. Stir together the sour cream and single cream in a mixing bowl, season with salt and stir to mix.

2 Add the Jerusalem artichokes to the cream and toss to coat evenly with the mixture. Spread the artichokes over the bottom of the prepared dish.

3 Sprinkle evenly with the cheese, then the breadcrumbs. Bake for about 30 minutes, until the cheese melts and the top is brown and bubbling.

Per portion Energy 296kcal/1230kJ; Protein 6.9g; Carbohydrate 27.6g, of which sugars 15.5g; Fat 18.1g, of which saturates 11.1g; Cholesterol 52mg; Calcium 186mg; Fibre 4.4g; Sodium 240mg.

Baked tomatoes with mint

This is a high summer recipe that makes the most of falling-off-the-vine ripe tomatoes and fresh mint. Serve this attractive dish with grilled lamb or fish. It is ideal for a barbecue.

Serves 4

6 large ripe tomatoes

300ml/½ pint/1¼ cups double (heavy) cream

2 sprigs of fresh mint

olive oil, for brushing

a few pinches of caster (superfine) sugar

30ml/2 tbsp grated Bonnet cheese

salt and ground black pepper

Cook's tip Bonnet is a hard variety of goat's cheese but any other hard, well-flavoured cheese will do.

1 Preheat the oven to 220°C/425°F/ Gas 7. Bring a pan of water to the boil and have a bowl of iced water ready. Cut the cores out of the tomatoes and make a cross at the base. Plunge the tomatoes into the boiling water for 10 seconds and then straight into the iced water. Leave to cool completely.

2 Put the cream and mint in a pan and bring to the boil. Reduce the heat and allow to simmer until it has reduced by about half.

3 Peel the cooled tomatoes and slice them thinly. Pat dry on kitchen paper.

4 Brush a shallow gratin dish lightly with a little olive oil. Layer the sliced tomatoes in the dish, overlapping slightly, and season with salt and ground black pepper. Sprinkle a little sugar over the top.

5 Strain the reduced cream evenly over the top of the tomatoes. Sprinkle on the cheese and bake in the preheated oven for 15 minutes, or until the top is browned and bubbling. Serve immediately in the gratin dish.

Per portion Energy 443kcal/1831kJ; Protein 5g; Carbohydrate 6.7g, of which sugars 6.7g; Fat 44.1g, of which saturates 27.4g; Cholesterol 113mg; Calcium 123mg; Fibre 1.8g; Sodium 105mg.

Oven-roast red onions

Serve these sticky, sweet and fragrant onions with roast chicken or warm as part of a mezze. Alternatively, crumble over some fresh herb cheese and serve with crusty bread.

Serves 4

4 large or 8 small red onions

45ml/3 tbsp olive oil

6 juniper berries, crushed

8 small rosemary sprigs

30ml/2 tbsp balsamic vinegar

salt and ground black pepper

Cook's tips
• To help hold back the tears, chill the onions first for about 30 minutes, then remove the root end last. The root contains the largest concentration of the sulphuric compounds that make the eyes water.
• If you don't have an onion baker, use a ceramic baking dish and cover with foil.

1 Soak a clay onion baker in cold water for 15 minutes, then drain. If the base of the baker is glazed, only the lid will need to be soaked.

2 Cut the onions from the tip to the root, cutting the large onions into quarters and the small onions in half. Trim the roots from the onions and remove the skins, if you like.

3 Rub the onions with olive oil, salt and pepper and the juniper berries. Place the onions in the baker, inserting the rosemary in among the onions. Pour the remaining olive oil and vinegar over.

4 Cover and place in an unheated oven. Set the oven to 200°C/400°F/Gas 6 and cook for 40 minutes. Remove the lid and cook for a further 10 minutes.

Per portion Energy 128kcal/530kJ; Protein 1.8g; Carbohydrate 11.9g, of which sugars 8.4g; Fat 8.6g, of which saturates 1.2g; Cholesterol 0mg; Calcium 38mg; Fibre 2.1g; Sodium 5mg.

Farmhouse cheese-baked courgettes

This is an easy dish that makes a great accompaniment to a wide range of meat and fish dishes or a good vegetarian lunch. Use piquant farmhouse cheddar or mature goat's cheese.

Serves 4

4 courgettes (zucchini)

30ml/2 tbsp grated hard farmhouse cheese, such as Gabriel or Desmond

about 25g/1oz/2 tbsp butter

salt and ground black pepper

1 Preheat the oven to 180°C/350°F/ Gas 4. Slice the courgettes in half, lengthways. Trim the ends and discard.

2 Butter a shallow baking dish and arrange the courgettes, cut side up, inside the dish.

3 Sprinkle the cheese over the courgettes, and sprinkle over a few knobs (pats) of butter. Bake in the preheated oven for about 20 minutes, or until the courgettes are tender and the cheese is bubbling and golden brown. Serve immediately.

Per portion Energy 96kcal/395kJ; Protein 3.8g; Carbohydrate 1.9g, of which sugars 1.8g; Fat 8g, of which saturates 5g; Cholesterol 21mg; Calcium 82mg; Fibre 0.9g; Sodium 93mg.

Greek courgette and potato bake

This is an early autumn dish known in Greece as Briami. Serve the oven-baked courgettes with bread, olives and grilled lamb, feta or halloumi cheese for a satisfying vegetarian meal.

Serves 6

675g/1½lb courgettes (zucchini)

450g/1lb potatoes, peeled and cut into chunks

1 onion, finely sliced

3 garlic cloves, chopped

1 large red (bell) pepper, seeded and cubed

400g/14oz can chopped tomatoes

150ml/¼ pint/⅔ cup extra virgin olive oil

150ml/¼ pint/⅔ cup hot water

5ml/1 tsp dried oregano

45ml/3 tbsp chopped fresh flat leaf parsley, plus a few extra sprigs, to garnish

salt and ground black pepper

1 Preheat the oven to 190°C/375°F/ Gas 5. Scrape the courgettes lightly under running water to dislodge any grit and then slice them into thin rounds. Put them in a large baking dish and add the chopped potatoes, onion, garlic, red pepper and tomatoes.

2 Mix well, then stir in the olive oil, hot water and dried oregano.

3 Spread the mixture evenly, then season with salt and pepper. Bake for 30 minutes, then stir in the parsley and a little more water.

4 Return to the oven and cook for 1 hour, increasing the temperature to 200°C/400°F/Gas 6 for the final 10–15 minutes, so that the potatoes brown.

Per portion Energy 374kcal/1,554kJ; Protein 6.6g; Carbohydrate 28.6g, of which sugars 11.2g; Fat 26.7g, of which saturates 4g; Cholesterol 0mg; Calcium 86mg; Fibre 5.1g; Sodium 29mg.

New potato salad with chives

The potatoes in this dish absorb the oil and vinegar dressing as they cool, and are then tossed in mayonnaise. Small waxy potatoes, which can be kept whole, are particularly suitable for this recipe. Serve them with cold poached salmon or roast chicken.

2 Meanwhile, finely chop the white parts of the spring onions together with a little of the green part.

3 Whisk the oil with the vinegar and mustard. Drain the potatoes. Immediately, while the potatoes are still hot and steaming, toss them lightly with the oil mixture and the spring onions. Leave to cool.

Serves 4–6

675g/1½lb small new potatoes, unpeeled

4 spring onions (scallions)

45ml/3 tbsp olive oil

15ml/1 tbsp cider vinegar or wine vinegar

2.5ml/½ tsp ready-made English (hot) mustard

175ml/6fl oz/¾ cup mayonnaise

45ml/3 tbsp chopped fresh chives

salt and ground black pepper

Variation Add a handful of chopped parsley or mint to the salad with the mayonnaise instead of chives.

1 Cook the new potatoes in boiling salted water for about 15 minutes, or until tender.

4 Stir the mayonnaise and chives into the cooled potatoes and turn into a serving bowl. Chill the salad until you are ready to serve.

Per portion Energy 182kcal/761kJ; Protein 2.5g; Carbohydrate 22.5g, of which sugars 1.9g; Fat 9.7g, of which saturates 1.5g; Cholesterol 0mg; Calcium 20mg; Fibre 1.7g; Sodium 17mg.

Blue cheese coleslaw

In this recipe, shredded crisp cabbage is tossed in a dressing flavoured with English blue cheese. White or red cabbage, or a mixture of the two, works well in this crunchy salad. Use a favourite blue cheese, and serve piled into hot baked potatoes or with roast chicken.

Serves 4–8

45ml/3 tbsp mayonnaise

45ml/3 tbsp thick natural (plain) yogurt

50g/2oz blue cheese, such as Stilton or Oxford Blue

15ml/1 tbsp lemon juice or cider vinegar

about 500g/1¼lb white cabbage

1 medium carrot

1 small red onion

2 small celery sticks

1 crisp eating apple

salt and ground black pepper

watercress sprigs, to garnish

2 Trim and shred the cabbage finely, grate the carrot, chop the onion finely and cut the celery into very thin slices. Core and dice the apple.

Variation Try making the coleslaw with a half-and-half mixture of red cabbage and white cabbage.

3 Add the cabbage, carrot, onion, celery and apple to the bowl and toss until all the ingredients are well mixed and coated with the dressing.

4 Cover the bowl and refrigerate for 2–3 hours or until ready to serve. Stir before serving; garnish with watercress.

1 To make the dressing, put the mayonnaise and yogurt into a large bowl and crumble in the cheese. Stir well, adding a squeeze of lemon juice and a little seasoning to taste.

Cook's tips
• Make the dressing by blending the ingredients in a food processor.
• If you have a slicing attachment, the cabbage can be finely shredded using a food processor.

Per portion Energy 86kcal/359kJ; Protein 2.7g; Carbohydrate 5.1g, of which sugars 4.8g; Fat 6.3g, of which saturates 1.9g; Cholesterol 9mg; Calcium 78mg; Fibre 1.6g; Sodium 116mg.

Puddings and desserts

The aroma of a gently steaming pudding is a delectable part of winter country cooking, while the abundant fruits of summer make luscious desserts. Rice puddings and fruit crumbles are nursery classics and, along with American pies, offer something for every sweet tooth. There are few simpler recipes than those for berry or rhubarb fools – they are easy to make and look very impressive.

Sticky honey and ginger baked apples

Baked apples are a country-cooking staple, and there are myriad different versions – they can be made with any type of eating apple and stuffed with vine fruits, spices and citrus fruits. This version uses honey and fresh ginger, and is accompanied by either vanilla sauce, sour cream or double cream. A final touch of luxury would be to fold a little whipped cream into the vanilla sauce before serving, then spooning stem ginger ice cream on top.

Serves 4

4 eating apples, such as Cox's Orange Pippin or Golden Delicious

30ml/2 tbsp finely chopped fresh root ginger

60ml/4 tbsp honey

25g/1oz/2 tbsp unsalted (sweet) butter

60ml/4 tbsp medium white wine

vanilla sauce, sour cream or double (heavy) cream, to serve

For the vanilla sauce

300ml/½ pint/1¼ cups single (light) cream

1 vanilla pod (bean), split lengthways

2 egg yolks

30ml/2 tbsp caster (superfine) sugar

1 To make the vanilla sauce, put the cream and vanilla pod in a pan and heat to just below boiling point. Remove from the heat and leave to infuse for 10 minutes. Remove the vanilla pod.

2 Put the egg yolks and sugar in a bowl and whisk them together until pale and thick, then slowly pour in the cream, whisking all the time.

3 Return the pan to the heat and heat very gently until the cream is thick enough to coat the back of a wooden spoon. (If you draw a finger horizontally across the back of the spoon, the sauce should be thick enough not to run down through the channel.)

4 Remove from the heat and leave to cool. Either stir from time to time, or cover to prevent a skin forming.

5 Preheat the oven to 160°C/325°F/ Gas 3. Remove the cores from the apples leaving the stalk end intact, but remove the actual stalk. Fill each cavity with 2.5ml/½ tbsp chopped ginger and 15ml/1 tbsp honey.

6 Place the apples in an ovenproof dish, with the open end uppermost, and top each one with a knob of butter.

7 Pour in the wine and bake in the oven, basting frequently with the cooking juices, for about 45 minutes, until the apples are tender. Serve the apples with the vanilla sauce, sour cream or double cream.

Cook's tip If the sauce looks as though it may overheat, plunge the base of the pan into a bowl of cold water. This will cool the contents and prevent it curdling.

Per portion Energy 331kcal/1381kJ; Protein 4.3g; Carbohydrate 27.8g, of which sugars 27.8g; Fat 22.3g, of which saturates 13.2g; Cholesterol 155mg; Calcium 89mg; Fibre 1.2g; Sodium 68mg.

Black cherry clafoutis

Clafoutis is a batter pudding that originated in the Limousin area of central France. It is often made with cream and traditionally uses slightly tart black cherries, although other soft fruits such as halved apricots, peaches or plums will also give delicious results.

Serves 6

butter, for greasing

450g/1lb/2 cups black cherries, pitted

25g/1oz/¼ cup plain (all-purpose) flour

50g/2oz/½ cup icing (confectioners') sugar, plus extra for dusting

4 eggs, beaten

250ml/8fl oz/1 cup full-cream (whole) milk

30ml/2 tbsp cherry liqueur, such as kirsch or maraschino

1 Preheat the oven to 180°C/350°F/ Gas 4. Generously grease a 1.2 litre/ 2 pint/5 cup dish and add the pitted black cherries.

2 Sift the flour and icing sugar into a large mixing bowl, then gradually whisk in the beaten eggs until the mixture is smooth. Whisk in the milk until well blended, then stir in the liqueur.

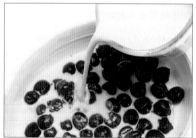

3 Pour the batter into the baking dish. Transfer to the oven and bake for about 40 minutes, or until just set and golden brown. Insert a knife into the centre of the pudding to test if it is cooked in the middle; the blade should come out clean.

4 Allow the pudding to cool for at least 15 minutes. Dust liberally with icing sugar just before serving, either warm or at room temperature.

Variations
• Try using other liqueurs – almond-flavoured liqueur is delicious teamed with cherries, while hazelnut, raspberry or orange liqueurs also work well.
• Also try other fruits, such as plums, apricots, blackberries or blueberries.

Per portion Energy 201kcal/843kJ; Protein 6.7g; Carbohydrate 23.8g, of which sugars 20.7g; Fat 8.9g, of which saturates 4.3g; Cholesterol 142mg; Calcium 89mg; Fibre 0.8g; Sodium 91mg.

Old-fashioned deep-dish apple pie

It is impossible to resist a really good home-baked apple pie. If you make your own shortcrust pastry and use eating apples bursting with flavour and loads of butter and sugar, you can't go wrong. Serve this old-fashioned dish with thick cream or nutmeg ice cream.

Serves 4

900g/2lb eating apples

75g/3oz/6 tbsp unsalted (sweet) butter

45–60ml/3–4 tbsp demerara
(raw) sugar

3 cloves

2.5ml/½ tsp mixed (apple pie) spice

For the pastry

250g/9oz/2¼ cups plain
(all-purpose) flour

pinch of salt

50g/2oz/¼ cup lard or white
cooking fat, chilled and diced

75g/3oz/6 tbsp unsalted butter,
chilled and diced

30–45ml/2–3 tbsp chilled water

a little milk, for brushing

caster (superfine) sugar, for dredging

clotted cream or ice cream, to serve

1 Preheat the oven to 200°C/400°F/Gas 6. Make the pastry first. Sift the flour and salt into a bowl. Rub in the lard or fat and butter. Stir in enough chilled water to bring the pastry together. Knead lightly, then wrap in clear film (plastic wrap) and chill for 30 minutes.

2 To make the filling, peel, core and thickly slice the apples. Melt the butter in a frying pan, add the sugar and cook for 3–4 minutes, allowing it to melt and caramelize. Add the apples and stir. Cook over a brisk heat until the apples take on a little colour, add the spices and tip out into a bowl to cool slightly.

3 Divide the pastry in two and, on a lightly floured surface, roll out into two rounds that will easily fit a deep 23cm/9in pie plate. Line the plate with one round of pastry. Spoon in the cooled filling and mound up in the centre.

4 Cover the apples with the remaining pastry, sealing and crimping the edges.

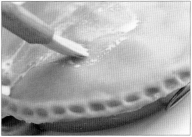

5 Make a 5cm/2in long slit through the top of the pastry to allow the steam to escape. Brush the pie with milk and dredge with caster sugar.

6 Place the pie on a baking sheet and bake in the oven for 25–35 minutes until golden and firm. Serve with dollops of thick cream or ice cream.

Per portion Energy 610kcal/2566kJ; Protein 8.1g; Carbohydrate 86.1g, of which sugars 40.2g; Fat 28.5g, of which saturates 8.8g; Cholesterol 14mg; Calcium 168mg; Fibre 8.1g; Sodium 413mg.

Peach and blueberry pie

With its attractive lattice pastry top, this colourful pie is bursting with plump blueberries and juicy peaches. It is good hot, or can be wrapped in its tin and transported to a picnic.

Serves 8

225g/8oz/2 cups plain (all-purpose) flour

2.5ml/½ tsp salt

5ml/1 tsp granulated (white) sugar

150g/5oz/10 tbsp cold butter or margarine, diced

1 egg yolk

30–45ml/2–3 tbsp iced water

30ml/2 tbsp milk, for glazing

For the filling

6 peaches, peeled, pitted and sliced

225g/8oz/2 cups fresh blueberries

150g/5oz/¾ cup granulated sugar

30ml/2 tbsp fresh lemon juice

40g/1½oz/⅓ cup plain (all-purpose) flour

pinch of grated nutmeg

25g/1oz/2 tbsp butter or margarine, cut into pea-size pieces

1 For the pastry, sift the flour, salt and sugar into a bowl. Rub the butter or margarine into the dry ingredients as quickly as possible until the mixture is crumbly and resembles breadcrumbs.

2 Mix the egg yolk with 30ml/2 tbsp of the iced water and sprinkle over the flour mixture. Combine with a fork until the pastry holds together. If the pastry is too crumbly, add a little more water, 5ml/1 tsp at a time. Gather the pastry into a ball and flatten into a disk. Wrap in clear film (plastic wrap) and chill for at least 20 minutes.

3 Roll out two-thirds of the pastry between two sheets of baking parchment to a thickness of about 3mm/⅛in. Use to line a 23cm/9in fluted tin (pan). Trim all around, leaving a 1cm/½in overhang, then trim the edges with a sharp knife.

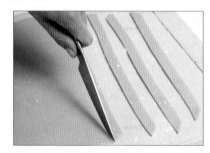

4 Gather the trimmings and remaining pastry into a ball, and roll out to a thickness of about 6mm/¼in. Using a pastry wheel or sharp knife, cut strips 1cm/½in wide. Chill the pastry case and the strips for 20 minutes. Preheat the oven to 200°C/400°F/ Gas 6.

5 Line the pastry case with baking parchment and fill with dried beans. Bake until the pastry case is just set, 12–15 minutes. Remove from the oven and carefully lift out the paper with the beans. Prick the bottom of the pastry case all over with a fork, then return to the oven and bake for 5 minutes more. Let the pastry case cool slightly before filling. Leave the oven on.

6 In a mixing bowl, combine the peach slices with the blueberries, sugar, lemon juice, flour and nutmeg. Spoon the fruit mixture evenly into the pastry case. Dot with the pieces of butter or margarine.

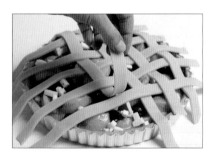

7 Weave a lattice top with the chilled pastry strips, pressing the ends to the baked pastry-case edge. Brush the strips with the milk.

8 Bake the pie for 15 minutes. Reduce the heat to 180°C/350°F/Gas 4, and continue baking until the filling is tender and bubbling and the pastry lattice is golden, about 30 minutes more. If the pastry gets too brown, cover loosely with a piece of foil. Serve the pie warm or at room temperature.

Cook's tip To peel stone (pit) fruits, place them in a large heat-proof bowl and cover with boiling water. Leave for 2–3 minutes until the skins wrinkle, then drain. The skin should slide off easily.

Per portion Energy 391kcal/1640kJ; Protein 4.7g; Carbohydrate 53g, of which sugars 27.7g; Fat 19.3g, of which saturates 11.7g; Cholesterol 72mg; Calcium 86mg; Fibre 2.9g; Sodium 139mg.

Boston cream pie

Actually a sponge cake filled with custard rather than cream and topped with a dark chocolate glaze, this cake is a reworking of the early American pudding cake pie.

Serves 8

225g/8oz/2 cups self-raising (self-rising) flour

15ml/1 tbsp baking powder

2.5ml/½ tsp salt

115g/4oz/½ cup butter, softened

200g/7oz/1 cup granulated (white) sugar

2 eggs

5ml/1 tsp vanilla extract

175ml/6fl oz/¾ cup milk

For the filling

250ml/8fl oz/1 cup milk

3 egg yolks

90g/3½oz/½ cup granulated (white) sugar

25g/1oz/¼ cup plain (all-purpose) flour

15g/½oz/1 tbsp butter

15ml/1 tbsp brandy or 5ml/1 tsp vanilla extract

For the chocolate glaze

25g/1oz cooking (unsweetened) chocolate

25g/1oz/2 tbsp butter or margarine

90g/3½oz/½ cup icing (confectioners') sugar, plus extra for dusting

2.5ml/½ tsp vanilla extract

about 15ml/1 tbsp hot water

1 Preheat the oven to 190°F/375°F/ Gas 5. Grease two 20cm/8in shallow round cake tins (pans), and line the bottoms with greased baking parchment.

2 Sift the flour with the baking powder and salt.

3 Beat the butter and granulated sugar together until light and fluffy. Add the eggs one at a time, beating well after each addition. Stir in the vanilla. Add the milk and dry ingredients alternately, mixing only enough to blend thoroughly. Do not over-beat the mixture.

4 Divide the mixture between the prepared tins and spread it out evenly. Bake until a skewer inserted in the centre comes out clean, about 25 minutes.

5 Meanwhile, make the filling. Heat the milk in a small pan to boiling point. Remove from the heat.

6 In a heatproof mixing bowl, beat the egg yolks. Gradually add the granulated sugar and continue beating until pale yellow. Beat in the flour.

7 Pour the hot milk into the egg yolk mixture in a steady stream, beating constantly. When all the milk has been added, place the bowl over a pan of boiling water, or pour the mixture into the top of a double boiler. Heat for 30 minutes, stirring constantly, until thickened. Remove from the heat. Stir in the butter and brandy or vanilla. Chill for 2–3 hours or until set.

8 When the cake layers have cooled, use a large sharp knife to slice off the domed top to make a flat surface. Place one layer on a serving plate and spread the filling on in a thick layer. Set the other layer on top, cut side down. Smooth the edge of the filling layer so it is flush with the sides of the cake layers.

9 For the glaze, melt the chocolate with the butter or margarine in the top of a double boiler, or in a bowl over hot water. When smooth, remove from the heat and beat in the sugar to make a thick paste. Add the vanilla. Beat in a little of the hot water. If the glaze does not have a spreadable consistency, add more water, 5ml/1 tsp at a time.

10 Spread the glaze evenly over the top of the cake, using a metal spatula. Dust the top with icing sugar. Because of the custard filling, any leftover cake must be chilled in the refrigerator, and can be stored for up to 3 days.

Per portion Energy 499kcal/2099kJ; Protein 6g; Carbohydrate 77g, of which sugars 53.1g; Fat 20.3g, of which saturates 12.1g; Cholesterol 146mg; Calcium 112mg; Fibre 1g; Sodium 296mg.

Poached spiced pears

The fragrant aroma of pears is greatly enhanced by gently poaching them in either spiced liquor or wine. Serve this dish warm or cold, with some cream whipped with icing sugar and Poire William, and perhaps some crisp, sweet biscuits to give a contrasting texture.

Serves 4

115g/4oz/½ cup caster (superfine) sugar

grated rind and juice of 1 lemon

2.5ml/½ tsp ground ginger

1 small cinnamon stick

2 whole cloves

4 firm ripe pears

Variations
• Omit the spices and instead flavour the water with ginger or elderflower cordial.
• Use white wine in place of water.

1 Put the sugar in a pan with 300ml/½ pint/1½ cups water, the lemon rind and juice, ginger and spices. Heat, stirring, until the sugar has dissolved.

2 Peel the pears, cut them in half lengthways and remove their cores.

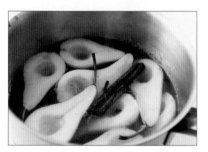

3 Add the pear halves to the pan and bring just to the boil. Cover and simmer gently for about 5 minutes or until the pears are tender, turning them over in the syrup occasionally during cooking. Remove from the heat and leave to cool in the syrup before serving.

Per portion Energy 93kcal/392kJ; Protein 0.5g; Carbohydrate 23.6g, of which sugars 23.6g; Fat 0.2g, of which saturates 0g; Cholesterol 0mg; Calcium 17mg; Fibre 3.3g; Sodium 6mg.

Chilled berry pudding

A cross between a summer pudding and a trifle, this fragrant, light pudding makes
the most of summer soft fruits and is a perfect summer dessert. Be sure to use a good
loaf of bread rather than processed sliced bread, to get the best texture and flavour.

Serves 1 6

550g/1lb 4oz mixed soft fruit,
such as raspberries, blackberries,
blackcurrants, redcurrants

50g/2oz/4 tbsp sugar

large thick slice of bread with crusts
removed, about 125g/4½oz/2 cups
without crusts

300ml/½ pint/1¼ cups double
(heavy) cream

45ml/3 tbsp elderflower cordial

150ml/¼ pint/⅔ cup thick natural
(plain) yogurt

Cook's tip During the seasons when
fresh summer fruits are not as readily
available, a bag of mixed frozen fruit
works just as well in this recipe.

1 Reserve a few raspberries, blackberries,
blackcurrants or redcurrants for
decoration, then put the remainder
into a pan with the sugar and
30ml/2 tbsp water. Bring just to
the boil, cover and simmer gently
for 4–5 minutes, until the fruit is
soft and plenty of juice has formed.

2 Cut the bread into cubes, measuring
about 2.5cm/1in, and put them into
one large dish or individual serving
bowls or glasses.

3 Spoon the fruit mixture over the
bread and leave to cool.

Variation Instead of mixing yogurt
into the topping, try using the same
quantity of ready-made custard – it
gives a richer, sweeter result to the
finished dish.

4 Whip the cream with the cordial
until stiff peaks begin to form. Gently
stir in the yogurt and spoon the
mixture over the top of the fruit.

5 Chill until required. Just before
serving, decorate the top with the
reserved fruit.

Per portion Energy 382kcal/1592kJ; Protein 5.2g; Carbohydrate 29.9g, of which sugars 20.2g; Fat 27.8g, of which saturates 16.9g; Cholesterol 69mg; Calcium 124mg; Fibre 2.6g; Sodium 144mg.

Gooseberry and elderflower fool

The combination of gooseberry and elderflower is heavenly, but rhubarb and ginger or raspberries are also classic ingredients for fruit fools – you can use whatever is ripe in the kitchen garden. Serve in pretty glasses, with crisp little biscuits to add a contrast of texture.

Serves 4

500g/1¼lb gooseberries

300ml/½ pint/1¼ cups double (heavy) cream

about 115g/4oz/1 cup icing (confectioners') sugar, to taste

30ml/2 tbsp elderflower cordial

mint sprigs, to decorate

crisp biscuits (cookies), to serve

1 Place the gooseberries in a heavy pan, cover and cook over a low heat, shaking the pan occasionally, until tender. Transfer the gooseberries into a bowl, crush them with a fork or potato masher, then leave to cool completely.

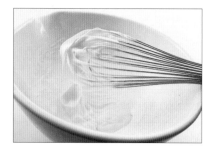

2 Whip the cream until soft peaks form, then fold in half the crushed fruit. Add sugar and elderflower cordial to taste. Sweeten the remaining fruit to taste.

3 Layer the cream mixture and the crushed gooseberries in four dessert dishes or tall glasses, then cover and chill until ready to serve. Decorate the fool with mint sprigs and serve with crisp sweet biscuits.

Variations
• When in season, cook 2–3 elderflower heads with the gooseberries and omit the elderflower cordial.
• For rhubarb fool use squeezed orange juice in place of elderflower cordial.

Per portion Energy 366kcal/1521kJ; Protein 3.5g; Carbohydrate 24.2g, of which sugars 21.8g; Fat 28.4g, of which saturates 16.7g; Cholesterol 70mg; Calcium 111mg; Fibre 1.9g; Sodium 41mg.

Rhubarb fool

This is a quick and simple dessert that makes the most of rhubarb when it is in season. You can use early or 'forced' rhubarb, which is a ravishing pink and needs very little cooking. Try adding a few drops of rosewater to the fruit as it cooks, and serve with shortbread.

1 Cut the rhubarb into pieces and wash thoroughly. Stew over a low heat with just the water clinging to it and the sugar. This takes about 10 minutes. Set aside to cool.

2 Pass the rhubarb through a fine sieve (strainer) so you have a thick purée.

3 Use equal parts of the purée, the whipped double cream and ready-made thick custard. Combine the purée and custard first, then fold in the cream. Chill in the refrigerator before serving. Serve with heather honey.

Serves 4

450g/1lb rhubarb, trimmed

75g/3oz/scant ½ cup soft light brown sugar

whipped double (heavy) cream and ready-made thick custard (see step 3)

Variations
• You can use another fruit if you like for this dessert – try bramble fruits or apples. Other stewed fruits also work well, such as prunes or peaches. For something a little more exotic, you could try mangoes.
• For a low-fat option, substitute natural (plain) yogurt for the cream.

Per portion Energy 439kcal/1828kJ; Protein 4.6g; Carbohydrate 34.1g, of which sugars 31.8g; Fat 31.7g, of which saturates 18.9g; Cholesterol 80mg; Calcium 233mg; Fibre 1.6g; Sodium 74mg.

Breads and baking

A country meal is not complete without a piece of bread, and there are few more welcoming aromas than a home-baked loaf. Doing your own baking can give great pleasure and satisfaction, and once the technique for basic dough has been mastered, there are endless variations and adaptations. Also in this chapter are recipes for biscuits, crumpets, scones and cakes – all essential country tea-time treats.

Poppyseed bloomer

This satisfying white poppyseed bread, which is a version of the chunky baton loaf found throughout Europe, is made using a slower rising method and with less yeast than usual. It produces a longer-keeping loaf with a fuller flavour. The dough takes about 8 hours to rise, so you'll need to start making the bread early in the morning.

Makes 1 large loaf

675g/1½ lb/6 cups unbleached white bread flour

10ml/2 tsp salt

15g/½ oz fresh yeast

430ml/15fl oz/1⅞ cups water

For the topping

2.5ml/½ tsp salt

30ml/2 tbsp water

poppy seeds, for sprinkling

Cook's tip You can get the cracked appearance of this loaf by spraying the oven with water before baking. If the underside is not crusty at the end, turn the loaf over, switch off the heat and leave in the oven for 5–10 minutes.

1 Lightly grease a baking sheet. Sift the flour and salt together into a large bowl and make a well in the centre.

2 Mix the yeast and 150ml/¼ pint/ ⅔ cup of the water in a bowl. Mix in the remaining water. Add to the centre of the flour. Mix, gradually incorporating the surrounding flour, until the mixture forms a firm dough.

3 Turn out on to a lightly floured surface and knead the dough for at least 10 minutes, until smooth and elastic. Place the dough in a lightly oiled bowl, cover with lightly oiled clear film (plastic wrap) and leave to rise, at cool room temperature, about 15–18°C/60–65°F, for 5–6 hours, or until doubled in bulk.

4 Knock back (punch down) the dough, turn out on to a lightly floured surface and knead it thoroughly and quite hard for about 5 minutes. Return the dough to the bowl, and re-cover. Leave to rise, at cool room temperature, for 2 hours.

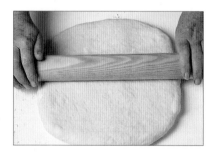

5 Knock back again and repeat the thorough kneading. Leave the dough to rest for 5 minutes, then roll out on a lightly floured surface into a rectangle 2.5cm/1in thick. Roll the dough up from one long side and shape it into a square-ended thick baton shape about 33 x 13cm/13 x 5in.

6 Place it seam side up on a lightly floured baking sheet, cover and leave to rest for 15 minutes. Turn the loaf over and place on the greased baking sheet. Plump up by tucking the dough under the sides and ends. Using a sharp knife, cut six diagonal slashes on the top.

7 Leave to rest, covered, in a warm place, for 10 minutes. Meanwhile preheat the oven to 230°C/450°F/Gas 8.

8 Mix the salt and water together and brush this glaze over the bread. Sprinkle with poppy seeds. Spray the oven with water, bake the bread immediately for 20 minutes, then reduce the oven temperature to 200°C/400°F/Gas 6. Bake for 25 minutes more, or until golden. Transfer to a wire rack to cool.

Variation You could also use sesame, cumin or nigella seeds instead of poppy seeds, or a mixture of seeds.

Per loaf Energy 2302kcal/9787kJ; Protein 63.5g; Carbohydrate 524.5g, of which sugars 10.1g; Fat 8.8g, of which saturates 1.3g; Cholesterol 0mg; Calcium 946mg; Fibre 20.9g; Sodium 3950mg.

Onion, olive and Parmesan bread

Versatile and delicious, this tasty bread is made with olive oil and cornmeal. Try it cut into chunks and dipped into olive oil. It is also wonderful as a base for bruschetta or filled with mozzarella and prosciutto, and makes delicious croûtons for tossing into a salad.

Makes 1 large loaf

350g/12oz/3 cups unbleached strong plain (all-purpose) flour, plus a little extra

115g/4oz/1 cup yellow cornmeal, plus a little extra

rounded 5ml/1 tsp salt

15g/½oz fresh yeast or 10ml/2 tsp active dried yeast

5ml/1 tsp muscovado (molasses) sugar

270ml/9fl oz/generous 1 cup warm water

5ml/1 tsp chopped fresh thyme

30ml/2 tbsp olive oil, plus a little extra for greasing

1 onion, finely chopped

75g/3oz/1 cup freshly grated Parmesan cheese

90g/3½oz/scant 1 cup pitted black olives, halved

1 Mix the flour, cornmeal and salt in a warmed bowl. If using fresh yeast, cream it with the sugar and gradually stir in 120ml/4fl oz/½ cup of the warm water. If using dried yeast, stir the sugar into the water and then sprinkle the dried yeast over the surface. Leave in a warm place for 10 minutes, until frothy.

2 Make a well in the centre of the dry ingredients and pour in the yeast liquid and a further 150ml/¼ pint/⅔ cup of the remaining warm water.

3 Add the chopped fresh thyme and 15ml/1 tbsp of the olive oil and mix thoroughly with a wooden spoon, gradually drawing in the dry ingredients until they are fully incorporated. Add a dash more warm water, if necessary, to make a soft, but not sticky, dough.

4 Knead the dough on a lightly floured work surface for 5 minutes, until smooth and elastic. Place in a clean, lightly oiled bowl and place in a polythene bag or cover with oiled clear film (plastic wrap). Set aside to rise in a warm, not hot place for 1–2 hours or until well risen.

5 Meanwhile, heat the remaining olive oil in a heavy frying pan. Add the onion and cook gently for 8 minutes, until softened. Set aside to cool.

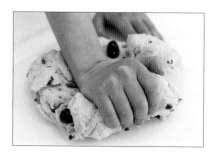

6 Brush a baking sheet with olive oil. Turn out the dough on to a floured work surface. Knead in the onions, followed by the Parmesan and olives.

7 Shape the dough into a rough oval loaf. Sprinkle a little cornmeal on the work surface and roll the bread in it, then place on the prepared baking sheet. Make several slits across the top.

8 Slip the baking sheet into the polythene bag or cover with oiled clear film and leave to rise in a warm place for about 1 hour, or until well risen.

9 Preheat the oven to 200°C/400°F/ Gas 6. Bake for 30–35 minutes, or until the bread sounds hollow when tapped on the base. Cool on a wire rack.

Variation Alternatively, shape the dough into a loaf, roll in cornmeal and place in an oiled loaf tin (pan). Leave to rise in the tin, then bake as in step 8.

Per loaf Energy 1142kcal/4803kJ; Protein 37.4g; Carbohydrate 182.5g, of which sugars 6.4g; Fat 32.5g, of which saturates 10.4g; Cholesterol 38mg; Calcium 733mg; Fibre 8.4g; Sodium 1428mg.

Plum and almond sponge cake

Seasonal country cooking is an obvious necessity in cold areas that have fierce extremes of climate. Traditionally, people ate what they could grow and stored food carefully to survive until the next harvest. Orchards have always been especially prized, and apple, pear and plum trees thrive in many cold countries. These fruits add sweetness, texture and variety to cakes. This sponge is best served warm and is equally good made with apricots or nectarines. The cardamom gives a hint of spice, which complements the fruit perfectly.

Serves 10

450g/1lb pitted fresh plums, coarsely chopped, plus 9 extra plums, stoned and halved, to decorate

300ml/½ pint/1¼ cups water

115g/4oz/½ cup unsalted (sweet) butter, softened

200g/7oz/1 cup caster (superfine) sugar

3 eggs

90g/3½oz/¾ cup toasted, finely chopped almonds

5ml/1 tsp bicarbonate of soda (baking soda)

7.5ml/1½ tsp baking powder

5ml/1 tsp ground cardamom

1.5ml/¼ tsp salt

250g/9oz/2¼ cups plain (all-purpose) flour

15ml/1 tbsp pearl sugar, to decorate

250ml/8fl oz/1 cup double (heavy) cream

10ml/2 tsp vanilla sugar

10ml/2 tsp icing (confectioners') sugar

Variation Pearl sugar – large crystals with a pearly sheen – is commonly used in Scandinavia to decorate pastries, buns and cakes. If you can't find it, use coarsely crushed white sugar cubes.

1 Place the chopped plums in a pan and add the water. Bring to the boil over a medium heat and cook for 10–15 minutes, until soft. Set aside to cool. You will need 350ml/12fl oz/1½ cups stewed plums for the cake.

2 Preheat the oven to 180°C/350°F/Gas 4. Grease and flour a 24cm/9½in springform cake tin (pan).

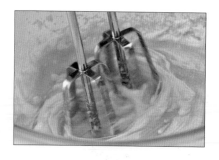

3 Cream the butter with the sugar in a mixing bowl until light and fluffy. Beat in the eggs, one at a time.

4 Stir in the stewed plums and the almonds. Add the baking soda, baking powder, cardamom and salt, and stir the mixture well together to distribute the fruit.

5 Gradually stir in the flour, a few spoons at a time, and mix until blended.

6 Pour the mixture into the prepared tin. Place 15 plum halves around the circumference of the cake and the remaining three halves in the centre, cut sides down. Sprinkle the pearl sugar over the cake.

7 Bake for 1 hour, or until the top springs back when lightly touched. Cool in the tin for 15 minutes before unfastening the ring.

8 Beat the double cream until soft peaks form. Stir in the vanilla sugar and the icing sugar and beat until thick. Serve the cake, still slightly warm, or at room temperature, in slices topped with a dollop of whipped cream.

Per portion Energy 311kcal/1308kJ; Protein 6.4g; Carbohydrate 44.5g, of which sugars 15.9g; Fat 13.2g, of which saturates 7.4g; Cholesterol 89mg; Calcium 86mg; Fibre 2.4g; Sodium 102mg.

Preserves, relishes and sauces

As well as preserving the taste of summer fruits and vegetables, it is immensely satisfying to make your own jams, jellies and relishes. Country-style home-made ones always taste better than store-bought varieties, and also make lovely gifts. Spicy and fruity relishes enliven the simplest of rustic dishes, and stirring a bubbling pot of preserves is a highly pleasurable rural pastime – both easy and rewarding.

Blackcurrant jam

Dark, jewelled blackcurrants look and taste fabulous in this classic fruity jam. Serve on hot buttered toast, crumpets or croissants, or use as a filling for cakes.

Makes about 1.3kg/3lb

1.3kg/3lb/12 cups blackcurrants

grated rind and juice of 1 orange

475ml/16fl oz/2 cups water

1.3kg/3lb/6½ cups granulated (white) sugar, warmed

30ml/2 tbsp cassis (optional)

1 Place the blackcurrants, orange rind and juice and water in a large heavy pan. Bring to the boil, reduce the heat and simmer for 30 minutes.

2 Add the warmed sugar to the pan and stir over a low heat until the sugar has dissolved.

3 Bring the mixture to the boil and cook for about 8 minutes, or until the jam reaches setting point (105°C/220°F).

4 Remove the pan from the heat and skim off any scum from the surface using a slotted spoon.

5 Leave to cool for 5 minutes, then stir in the cassis, if using.

6 Pour the jam into warmed sterilized jars and seal. Leave the jars to cool completely, then label and store in a cool, dark place. The jam will keep for up to 6 months.

Per portion Energy 5504kcal/23,503kJ; Protein 18.4g; Carbohydrate 1448.7g, of which sugars 1448.7g; Fat 0.1g, of which saturates 0g; Cholesterol 0mg; Calcium 1474mg; Fibre 46.9g; Sodium 122mg.

Cherry berry conserve

Tart cranberries add an extra dimension to this delicious berry conserve. It is perfect for adding to sweet sauces, serving with roast duck, or for simply spreading on hot crumpets.

1 Put the cranberries in a food processor and process until coarsely chopped. Scrape into a pan and add the cherries, fruit syrup and lemon juice.

2 Add the water to the pan. Cover and bring to the boil, then simmer for 20–30 minutes, or until the cranberries are very tender.

3 Add the sugar to the pan and heat gently, stirring, until the sugar has dissolved. Bring to the boil, then cook for 10 minutes, or to setting point (105°C/220°F).

4 Remove the pan from the heat and skim off and discard any scum using a slotted spoon. Leave to cool for 10 minutes, then stir gently and pour into warmed sterilized jars. Seal, label and store in a cool, dark place.

Cook's tip The cranberries must be cooked until very tender before the sugar is added, otherwise they will become tough.

Makes about 1.3kg/3lb

350g/12oz/3 cups fresh cranberries

1kg/2¼lb/5½ cups cherries, pitted

120ml/4fl oz/½ cup blackcurrant or raspberry syrup

juice of 2 lemons

250ml/8fl oz/1 cup water

1.3kg/3lb/6½ cups preserving or granulated (white) sugar, warmed

Per portion Energy 5859kcal/24,986kJ; Protein 16.7g; Carbohydrate 1540.4g, of which sugars 1540.4g; Fat 1.4g, of which saturates 0g; Cholesterol 0mg; Calcium 844mg; Fibre 14.6g; Sodium 105mg.

Hedgerow jelly

In the autumn, foraged hedgerow fruits such as damsons, blackberries and elderberries are wonderful for this delightful country jelly. Serve with cold meats or cheese.

Makes about 1.3kg/3lb

450g/1lb damsons, washed

450g/1lb/4 cups blackberries, washed

225g/8oz/2 cups raspberries

225g/8oz/2 cups elderberries, washed

juice and pips (seeds) of 2 large lemons

about 1.3kg/3lb/6½ cups preserving or granulated (white) sugar, warmed

1 Put the fruit, lemon juice and pips in a large pan. Add water to just below the level of the fruit. Cover and simmer for 1 hour. Mash the fruit, then leave to cool slightly.

2 Pour into a scalded jelly bag suspended over a non-metallic bowl and leave to drain overnight. Don't squeeze the bag as this will cloud the jelly.

3 Measure the strained juice into a preserving pan. Add 450g/1lb/ 2¼ cups sugar for every 600ml/ 1 pint/2½ cups strained fruit juice.

4 Heat the mixture, stirring, over a low heat until the sugar has dissolved.

5 Increase the heat and boil rapidly without stirring for 10–15 minutes, or until the jelly reaches setting point (105°C/220°F).

6 Remove the pan from the heat and skim off any scum using a slotted spoon.

7 Ladle into warmed, sterilized jars and seal. Leave to cool, then label and store for up to 6 months.

Per portion Energy 5229kcal/22,306kJ; Protein 9.3g; Carbohydrate 1382.8g, of which sugars 1382.8g; Fat 0.4g, of which saturates 0g; Cholesterol 0mg; Calcium 799mg; Fibre 8.6g; Sodium 86mg.

Spiced cider jelly

This wonderfully spicy jelly goes well with cheese and crackers, or can simply be spread on to warm toast. It is also good spooned into rice pudding or added to apple pie filling.

Makes about 1.3kg/3lb

900g/2lb tart cooking apples, washed and coarsely chopped, with skins and cores intact

900ml/1¼ pints/3¾ cups sweet cider

juice and pips (seeds) of 2 oranges

1 cinnamon stick

6 whole cloves

150ml/½ pint/⅔ cup water

about 900g/2lb/4½ cups preserving or granulated (white) sugar, warmed

1 Put the apples, cider, juice and pips, cinnamon, cloves and water in a large pan. Bring to the boil, cover and simmer for about 1 hour.

2 Leave to cool slightly, then pour the fruit into a scalded jelly bag suspended over a non-metallic bowl and leave to drain overnight.

3 Measure the strained juice into a preserving pan. Add 450g/1lb/ 2¼ cups warmed sugar for every 600ml/1 pint/2½ cups juice.

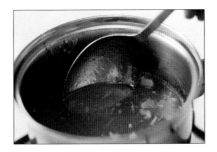

4 Heat, stirring, over a low heat until the sugar has dissolved. Increase the heat and boil, without stirring, for 10 minutes, or until the jelly reaches setting point (105°C/220°F).

5 Remove from the heat and skim off any scum. Ladle into warmed sterilized jars. Leave to cool, then cover, seal and label the jars. Store in a dark cupboard for up to 6 months.

Per portion Energy 3975kcal/16,950kJ; Protein 5.4g; Carbohydrate 990.6g, of which sugars 990.6g; Fat 0.3g, of which saturates 0g; Cholesterol 0mg; Calcium 561mg; Fibre 4.8g; Sodium 123mg.

Sweet piccalilli

Undoubtedly one of the most popular relishes, piccalilli can be eaten with grilled sausages, ham, chops or cold meats, or a strong, well-flavoured cheese such as Cheddar. It should contain a good selection of fresh, crunchy vegetables in a smooth mustard sauce.

Makes about 1.8kg/4lb

1 large cauliflower

450g/1lb pickling (pearl) onions

900g/2lb mixed vegetables,
such as marrow (large zucchini),
cucumber, French (green) beans

225g/8oz/1 cup salt

2.4 litres/4 pints/10 cups cold water

200g/7oz/1 cup granulated
(white) sugar

2 garlic cloves, peeled and crushed

10ml/2 tsp mustard powder

5ml/1 tsp ground ginger

1 litre/1¾ pints/4 cups distilled
(white) vinegar

25g/1oz/¼ cup plain
(all-purpose) flour

15ml/1 tbsp turmeric

Cook's tip Traditional preserving pans are copper, but if you don't have a preserving pan, any stainless steel, shallow and wide-topped pan will be suitable – this will aid evaporation and give a good result.

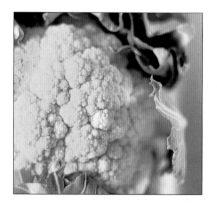

1 Prepare the vegetables. Divide the cauliflower into small florets; peel and quarter the pickling onions; seed and finely dice the marrow and cucumber; top and tail the French beans, then cut them into 2.5cm/1in lengths.

2 Layer the vegetables in a large glass or stainless steel bowl, generously sprinkling each layer with salt. Pour over the water, cover the bowl with clear film (plastic wrap) and leave to soak for about 24 hours.

3 Drain the soaked vegetables and discard the brine. Rinse well in several changes of cold water to remove as much salt as possible, then drain them thoroughly.

4 Put the sugar, garlic, mustard, ginger and 900ml/1½ pints/3¾ cups of the vinegar in a preserving pan. Heat gently, stirring occasionally, until the sugar has dissolved.

5 Add the vegetables to the pan, bring to the boil, reduce the heat and simmer for 10–15 minutes, or until they are almost tender.

6 Mix the flour and turmeric with the remaining vinegar and stir into the vegetables. Bring to the boil, stirring, and simmer for 5 minutes, until the piccalilli is thick.

7 Spoon the piccalilli into warmed sterilized jars, cover and seal. Store in a cool, dark place for at least 2 weeks. Use within 1 year.

Per portion Energy 1358kcal/5757kJ; Protein 34.1g; Carbohydrate 300.8g, of which sugars 266g; Fat 12g, of which saturates 1.2g; Cholesterol 0mg; Calcium 555mg; Fibre 20.6g; Sodium 4011mg.

Green tomato chutney

This is a classic chutney for using the last tomatoes of summer that just never seem to ripen. Apples and onions contribute essential flavour, which is enhanced by the addition of spice. This zesty chutney is good in sandwiches, for barbecues and with burgers.

Makes about 2.5kg/5½lb

1.8kg/4lb green tomatoes, chopped

450g/1lb cooking apples, peeled, cored and chopped

450g/1lb onions, chopped

2 large garlic cloves, crushed

15ml/1 tbsp salt

45ml/3 tbsp pickling spice

600ml/1 pint/2½ cups cider vinegar

450g/1lb/2¼ cups granulated (white) sugar

1 Place the tomatoes, apples, onions and garlic in a large pan and add the salt.

2 Tie the pickling spice in a piece of muslin (cheesecloth) and add to the ingredients in the pan.

3 Add half the vinegar to the pan and bring to the boil. Reduce the heat, then simmer for 1 hour, or until the chutney is reduced and thick, stirring frequently.

4 Put the sugar and remaining vinegar in a pan and heat gently until the sugar has dissolved, then add to the chutney. Simmer for 1½ hours until thick, stirring the mixture occasionally.

5 Remove the muslin bag from the chutney, then spoon the hot chutney into warmed sterilized jars. Cover and seal immediately. Allow the chutney to mature for at least 1 month before using.

Per portion Energy 2398kcal/10,233kJ; Protein 21.6g; Carbohydrate 601.7g, of which sugars 591.3g; Fat 6.8g, of which saturates 1.8g; Cholesterol 0mg; Calcium 495mg; Fibre 31.5g; Sodium 2177mg.

Plum and cherry relish

This simple sweet-and-sour fruit relish complements rich poultry, game or meat, such as roast duck or grilled duck breasts. You can sieve a few spoonfuls into a sauce or gravy to give fruity zest and flavour, as well as adding an appetizing splash of bright red colour.

1 Halve and pit the plums, then roughly chop the flesh. Pit all the cherries and cut them in half.

2 Cook the shallots gently in the oil for 5 minutes, or until soft. Add the fruit, sherry, vinegars, bay leaf and sugar.

3 Slowly bring the mixture to the boil, stirring until the sugar has dissolved completely. Increase the heat and cook briskly for about 15 minutes, or until the relish is very thick and the fruit tender.

4 Remove the bay leaf and spoon the relish into warmed sterilized jars. Cover and seal. Store the relish in the refrigerator and use within 3 months.

Makes about 350g/12oz

350g/12oz dark-skinned red plums

350g/12oz/2 cups cherries

2 shallots, finely chopped

15ml/1 tbsp olive oil

30ml/2 tbsp dry sherry

60ml/4 tbsp red wine vinegar

15ml/1 tbsp balsamic vinegar

1 bay leaf

90g/3½oz/scant ½ cup demerara (raw) sugar

Cook's tip Use a large preserving pan in which the mixture comes only half-way up the side. Always use just-ripe or slightly under-ripe fruits, as the pectin levels reduce when the fruit ripens. Pectin is essential to achieve a good set.

Per portion Energy 804kcal/3407kJ; Protein 6.5g; Carbohydrate 170.3g, of which sugars 168.9g; Fat 11.8g, of which saturates 1.6g; Cholesterol 0mg; Calcium 156mg; Fibre 9.6g; Sodium 21mg.

Mint sauce

In England, mint sauce is the traditional and inseparable accompaniment to roast lamb. Its fresh tart and astringent flavour is the perfect foil to rich, strongly flavoured lamb. As well as being extremely simple to make, it is infinitely superior to the store-bought varieties.

Makes about 250ml/8fl oz/1cup

1 large bunch mint

105ml/7 tbsp boiling water

150ml/¼ pint/⅔ cup wine vinegar

30ml/2 tbsp granulated (white) sugar

Cook's tip To make a quick and speedy Indian raita for serving with crispy poppadums, simply stir a little mint sauce into a small bowl of natural (plain) yogurt. Serve the raita alongside a bowl of tangy mango chutney.

1 Using a sharp knife, chop the mint very finely and place it in a 600ml/ 1 pint/2½ cup jug (pitcher). Pour the boiling water over the mint and leave to infuse for about 10 minutes.

2 When the mint infusion has cooled and is lukewarm, stir in the wine vinegar and sugar. Continue stirring (but do not mash up the mint leaves) until the sugar has dissolved completely.

3 Pour the mint sauce into a warmed sterilized bottle or jar. Seal the jar, label it with the date and store in the refrigerator or a cool, dark place.

Cook's tip This mint sauce can keep for up to 6 months when stored in the refrigerator, but is best when used within 3 weeks.

Per portion Energy 161kcal/685kJ; Protein 3.9g; Carbohydrate 36.6g, of which sugars 31.3g; Fat 0.7g, of which saturates 0g; Cholesterol 0mg; Calcium 226mg; Fibre 0g; Sodium 17mg.

Real horseradish sauce

Fiery, peppery horseradish sauce is without doubt the essential accompaniment to roast beef, and is also delicious served with smoked salmon. Horseradish, like chilli, is a powerful ingredient, so take care when handling it, and always wash your hands afterwards.

Makes about 200ml/7fl oz/scant 1 cup

45ml/3 tbsp freshly grated horseradish root

15ml/1 tbsp white wine vinegar

5ml/1 tsp granulated (white) sugar

pinch of salt

150ml/¼ pint/⅔ cup thick double (heavy) cream, for serving

Cook's tip To counteract the potent fumes of the horseradish, keep the root submerged in water while you chop and peel it. Use a food processor to do the fine chopping or grating, and avert your head when removing the lid.

1 Place the grated horseradish in a bowl, then add the white wine vinegar, granulated sugar and just a pinch of salt.

2 Stir the ingredients together, mixing them well until they are thoroughly combined and smooth.

3 Pour the mixture into a sterilized jar. It will keep in the refrigerator for up to 6 months.

4 A few hours before you intend to serve the sauce, stir the cream into the horseradish and leave to infuse. Stir once again before serving.

Per portion Energy 774kcal/3190kJ; Protein 2.8g; Carbohydrate 9.9g, of which sugars 9.8g; Fat 80.7g, of which saturates 50.1g; Cholesterol 206mg; Calcium 98mg; Fibre 1.1g; Sodium 40mg.

Moutarde aux fines herbes

This fragrant, hot mustard may be used either as a delicious condiment or for coating meats such as chicken and pork, or oily fish such as mackerel, before cooking. It is also fabulous when smeared thinly on cheese on toast, for an added bite.

Makes about 300ml/½ pint/1¼ cups

75g/3oz/scant ½ cup white mustard seeds

50g/2oz/¼ cup soft light brown sugar

5ml/1 tsp salt

5ml/1 tsp whole peppercorns

2.5ml/½ tsp ground turmeric

200ml/7fl oz/scant 1 cup distilled malt vinegar

60ml/4 tbsp chopped fresh mixed herbs, such as parsley, sage, thyme and rosemary

1 Put the mustard seeds, sugar, salt, whole peppercorns and ground turmeric into a food processor or blender and process for about 1 minute, or until the peppercorns are coarsely chopped.

2 Gradually add the vinegar to the mustard mixture, 15ml/1 tbsp at a time, processing well between each addition, then continue processing until a coarse paste forms.

3 Add the chopped fresh herbs to the mustard and mix well, then leave to stand for 10–15 minutes until the mustard thickens slightly.

4 Spoon the mustard into a 300ml/½ pint/1¼ cup sterilized jar. Cover the surface of the mustard with a baking parchment disc, then seal with a screw-top lid or a cork, and label. Store in a cool, dark place for up to 3 months.

Per portion Energy 553kcal/2324kJ; Protein 23.4g; Carbohydrate 69.1g, of which sugars 53.4g; Fat 34.5g, of which saturates 1.1g; Cholesterol 3mg; Calcium 374mg; Fibre 2.5g; Sodium 23mg.

Honey mustard

Delicious home-made mustards mature to make the most aromatic of condiments. This honey mustard is richly flavoured and is wonderful served with meats and cheeses, or stirred into sauces and salad dressings to give an extra peppery bite. The addition of honey gives a sweet counterbalance to the hot mustard seeds.

Makes about 500g/1¼b

225g/8oz/1 cup mustard seeds

15ml/1 tbsp ground cinnamon

2.5ml/½ tsp ground ginger

300ml/½ pint/1½ cups white wine vinegar

90ml/6 tbsp dark clear honey

Cook's tip Use well-flavoured clear honey for this recipe. Set (crystallized) honey does not have the right consistency and will not work well.

1 Put the mustard seeds in a bowl with the cinnamon and ginger, and pour over the white wine vinegar. Stir well to mix, then cover and leave to soak overnight in a cool place.

2 The next day, put the mustard mixture in a mortar and pound with a pestle, adding the honey very gradually.

3 Continue pounding and mixing until the mustard resembles a stiff paste. If the mixture becomes too stiff, add a little extra vinegar to achieve the desired consistency.

4 Spoon the mustard into four warmed sterilized jars. Seal and label the jars, then store in a cool, dark place or in the refrigerator. Keep refrigerated after opening, and use within 4 weeks.

Per portion Energy 1276kcal/5345kJ; Protein 65.4g; Carbohydrate 115.3g, of which sugars 68.8g; Fat 101.5g, of which saturates 3.4g; Cholesterol 9mg; Calcium 747mg; Fibre 0g; Sodium 21mg.

Index

Picture acknowledgements

t=top, b=bottom, l=left, r=right
iStockphoto: 11t, 27b, 28t,
29tl, 29tr, 32bl.